Emma Martin Marshall

In the Choir of Westminster Abbey

Emma Martin Marshall

In the Choir of Westminster Abbey

ISBN/EAN: 9783744661737

Printed in Europe, USA, Canada, Australia, Japan

Cover: Foto ©Thomas Meinert / pixelio.de

More available books at **www.hansebooks.com**

IN THE CHOIR
OF WESTMINSTER ABBEY

A STORY OF HENRY PURCELL'S DAYS

BY

EMMA MARSHALL

Author of ' Under Salisbury Spire,' ' Kensington Palace,'
' The Master of the Musicians,' Etc.

With Illustrations by

T. HAMILTON CRAWFORD, R.S.W.

THIRD EDITION

LONDON
SEELEY AND CO. LIMITED
38 GREAT RUSSELL STREET
1899

I AM indebted to the *Life of Purcell* by Mr Cummings for many of the incidents related in connection with him in this story.

Mr Gosse's *Life of Congreve* has also been consulted, with such contemporary history of the Revolution of 1688 and accession of William and Mary as bore upon the musical compositions of the great organist of Westminster Abbey.

WOODSIDE, LEIGH WOODS, CLIFTON,
September 1897.

LIST OF ILLUSTRATIONS

In the Choir of Westminster Abbey

CHAPTER I

A.D. 1684

As I look back on my past life, I may say it has been uneventful, yet it has fallen to my lot to see and hear much regarding those whose names are famous. So, mayhap, the record, which is a pleasing occupation to write, will be of interest to my descendants when I have passed hence.

There comes to most of us a time of awakening from the dreams of childhood, a time when the shadows and bright visions of youth change into realities—times when we are brought face to face with the conviction that our pathway is not always flower-strewn, but there are thorns and brambles to encounter, and rough places to pass over, which cannot be avoided.

3

Such an awakening came to me on a spring day in the year of grace 1684. The harsh voice of my stepmother called me from the poultry-yard, where I was feeding the pigeons, and singing to myself as I scattered the grain for the pretty creatures, who came down from the dove-cot, preening their feathers and strutting hither and thither as they pecked and cooed at my feet, for they knew me, and counted me as a friend.

'Betty!'—the call was repeated—'come this instant; you are wanted—Betty!' I had a perverse desire never to hurry when my stepmother called me in threatening tones. So I walked leisurely enow to the gate of the yard, and saw my stepmother standing at the back door of our low-roofed house, repeating, 'Betty, you tiresome nussy! go and smooth your tangled hair, and put on a clean cap, for a gentleman wants to see you. You are not well favoured, I can tell you, and had need make the best of yourself. You are no beauty, and a sad slattern.'

I had heard this many a time, and was not greatly moved by it. I lived my own life apart from my stepmother and her children. Certain it is I gave her no cause to love me, and was, I well believe, far from trying to win her favour.

How it was my poor father married a shrew, who brought four children by her first husband, as well as an orphan nephew of his—by name Edmund Pelham—I cannot tell.

It is ever a mystery why sharp-tongued women manage to get husbands over whom they ride rough-shod, while many a gentle one is left unwooed and unwed. It would seem that vixens win in the long run, and get men to marry them by hook or by crook. Witness my stepmother, who had had two husbands, and was ready for a third—if he presented himself.

I went up to my garret in the roof and did my stepmother's bidding. I had, as she said, tangled hair, but I thrust it back under the best cap which I wore on Sundays, tied with cherry-coloured riband, and let down my skirt, which was pulled through the pocket holes to keep it out of the way when about my work in the poultry-yard and dairy, and tied on a clean apron with a bib to hide blemishes, and so went to the parlour.

'Oh! is this the girl, Mistress Lockwood? And you want to get rid of her—eh?'

'Make your curtsey, Betty. This is his reverence, Master William Gostling, who is so condescending as to wish to see you.'

I felt a pair of keen eyes were looking at me

from head to foot. Then Mr Gostling said with
a kindly smile,—

'Stepmother and you don't agree, and you won't
break your hearts if you part company?'

'I'll answer for myself,' my stepmother said, 'and
I shall be thankful if Betty is a good girl and earns
her bread. I have much ado to live, with four
of my own children to feed and clothe; and a
strapping lass like Betty should better herself if
the chance comes in her way. She is mostly in
a dream here, and full of vagaries.'

'That won't answer for the place I have in view
for her. No dreaming and no vagaries, but quick-
ness and diligence and readiness to serve. But
come hither, Betty,' Mr Gostling said, 'and tell me
your mind.'

I curtseyed and said,—

'First, sir, an it pleases you, I must know yours.'

A pleasant smile broke over the face, which was
bent towards me.

'That's just and proper. So now I will tell you
all I have to tell. I have a dear friend, by name
Master Henry Purcell, who lives in Dean's Yard,
Westminster. His good wife needs help in the
household—not menial service, but help. Moreover, there is a great deal of copying music to
be done, mechanical work, needing neatness and

precision. Do you take to this offer? If so, I
shall, so I hope, do you and my friend a kindness,
and a kindness to one whom I held in high esteem
—your dead mother.'

'Oh! sir,' I exclaimed, 'if you knew her'— and
then I was choked with tears.

'Yes, yes, I knew her; a fair, sweet creature, with
the voice of an angel, and of gentle birth. You do
not resemble her except in the tones of your voice.'

And here my stepmother interrupted.

'I've oftentimes heard Betty's father say she
favoured him and not her mother; but she has
got her vagaries from her, for the poor thing
never knew whether she was on her head or her
heels!'

'Tut! tut! Mistress Lockwood,' Mr Gostling
said, bristling up, 'methinks it is ill-spoken to dis-
parage the dead. Whatsoever Frances Lockwood
did, she was an angel of goodness.'

My stepmother, fearful of offending Mr Gostling,
hastened to draw back her words, and declared
she knew my mother, and that she was all Mr
Gostling said she was.

'Oh! sir,' I ventured to say, 'I am not wanted
here. I pray you let me go to your friends. I
will do my utmost, I will indeed.'

Even now I can recall the thrill of delight with

which I felt the hand of Mr Gostling laid on my shoulder as he said,—

'Well, you shall make a trial of this, at anyrate, and get yourself ready to start by the stage-waggon which passes this way by the Tuesday in next week. I will meet you at the hostel where the stage puts down its passengers, and take you to Dean's Yard. Do you love music?'

Now, I had only heard the bassoon and fiddle in our village church, and yet music was in my soul, else how was it the song of the birds, the ripple of the mill stream, the whisper of the wind often moved me to ecstasy.

I've lain many a time listening to the sounds around me, and longing, longing to keep ever in the enchanted ground they made for me. Thus, as I say, I had lived my life apart for sixteen years, with but scant knowledge of what was passing around me, weary of the spoiled, unruly children, doing little services, such as skimming the milk in the dairy and feeding the pigeons, in a desultory way. But to Mr Gostling's question, Do you love music? put in the deep bass voice, such as, sure, there never was one deeper, I answered,—

'Yes, sir: I know I do; though I have never heard any except—'

I stopped, it seemed so strange to say I loved what I had never heard.

'Except what, child? Speak out.'

'Except the music that is all around me—the music of the birds, and the dripping water, and the wind.'

'There, that will do, that will do. You will soon know what music is when once you have listened to Master Purcell on the organ; you will hear in it, as he calls it forth, the wind and the waves, and all the hundred voices which are, with due reverence let me say it, as the voice of God to the soul of man.'

Mr Gostling and I were left alone in the parlour while my stepmother went to fetch a tankard of spiced canary and some sweet biscuits from the buttery for his refreshment.

'You will not be sorry to leave your home? Mistress Lockwood told a friend of mine in Canterbury that she wished to find you a place in some gentleman's family, for she was put to it for money. This seems strange.'

'Indeed it is strange, sir, for it is all my father's money. She has none, save what he left her; and yet she has grudged me my fare, and had it not been for Edmund Pelham, I should never have had a book or learned aught. He has come hither from his

college, and he has brought me books and taught
me a little Latin, and has bid me take heart, for
the longest lane has a turning.'

Mr Gostling laughed.

' Yours has been but a short lane, child, and I fear
me you have lacked patience, but I look to you to
fulfil the duties which fall to you in Master Purcell's household. No dreaming, you understand—
no vagaries—though I scarce know what Mistress
Lockwood means by this.'

My stepmother returned now with the silver cup
and biscuits, followed by Tommy, the youngest
of her children, who, unmannerly child as he was,
stretched out a greedy hand and half cleared the
platter of the cakes. His mother boxed his ears,
but he only grinned and scampered off to the orchard, from which we soon heard cries and quarrels,
and I knew it was no doubt because his sister
Madge would fain share his prize.

I counted the days and hours till Tuesday, and
set about my preparations with a will. Strange to
say, my stepmother was for once kinder than her
wont. She brought out some taffeta and lace which
had been my own mother's, and she gave me a small
oaken chest to hold my best attire, instead of rolling
it up in a package, which travelling on horseback
made necessary.

The evening before my departure I was surprised to see Edmund Pelham come up the garden path. He found me in the porch. My stepmother had gone into the village with Madge and Tommy, and I was free to sit quiet and try to fancy what my future life would be.

'Hallo, little Bet! at the old game—moping by yourself. I am on my way to present myself for a tutor's place at Eastham, and thought I would look in on my way. I came on foot from Cambridge, and I am dead tired.' He threw himself down on the floor of the porch at my feet, and asked, 'How goes the *Faërie Queen*, and what think you of Shakespeare's sonnets?'

'I have got some of them by heart,' I said; 'but, Edmund, I am going away from home; you are only just in time. I start by the stage-waggon on the morrow.'

'Going away!—that's bad news. Has she been more vicious than usual?'

'No; kinder. It is nought to do with her this time, except that she made it known to some gossips of hers in Canterbury that it was time I earned my bread.'

Edmund started up.

'Shame!' he cried; 'your father never made his will as he should have done, but he trusted to

madam to see you well provided for. Earn your
bread, forsooth! Why, you should have the best
to be had here. Is it all spending on those
brats?'

'She has to pay Dick and Harry's schooling at
Hitchin, and two of the milch cows got a dis-
temper and died, and oh! she says she can scarce
pay her way. But, Edmund, I am well pleased to
go. I am not wanted here, nor loved, nor cared
for. It is best for me to go.'

'And, pray, where are you going?'

'To Westminster, to live with Mistress Purcell.'

'What! the wife of the great musician everyone
is beginning to talk of?'

'Yes; Master Gostling is Master Purcell's friend,
and he it is who has furthered the scheme.'

'That sounds a better plan than I had feared.
Yet, Betty, it is ill done to turn you out from Ivy
Farm—from your home.'

'It has not been like home since Madam Lockwood came into it. If it had not been for you, I
should have had no friend here. It is, as I say,
quite the best thing that I should go.'

'Well, it may be so, but if you are not happy at
Westminster, let me know. I intend to get up in
the world, and if I do, you shall rise with me—eh,
Betty?'

'Time enough to think of that,' I said.

'I have taken my degree at Cambridge, and I mean to get to the Bar. Meanwhile, to keep my head above water, I shall get the care of a dunderhead to try and drive some Latin and Greek into his head. He is the only son of a pair of doting parents, Sir William and my Lady Audrey Wilmot. I shall enter at the Temple all the same, and eat my dinners and see you when I come to do this, so you won't be quite rid of me, little Bet!'

'As if I wished to be rid of the only friend I have in the wide world!' I answered.

I remember now, as if 'twere yesterday, how Edmund looked up into my face as he lay at my feet, and, taking my hand, said,—

'I will not bind you, Betty, with any promise, but I swear that nought shall turn my heart from you, and when I rise, as rise I *will*, if you consent, you shall share my good fortune.'

'You will find someone else by that time,' I said. 'You will see a fair lady who will be proud to have you for a suitor, and then you will wonder you ever cared for me. I am no beauty — my stepmother is right in that.'

'And I vow she is wrong. Were ever eyes like yours, Bet? They are like nothing in the world so much as the brown pool by the mill—brown but clear in its cool depths. And then your hair —how it ripples in the sunshine!'

'And then my short nose,' I said, laughing, 'which turns upwards, I am afraid; and my large mouth and my sallow cheeks.'

I spoke in jest, for I did not wish Edmund to know how in my secret heart I was thrilled with his words, and that I knew now for the first time that I loved him—him only!

I was only just past my sixteenth birthday, and he was twenty-three. Was it likely he would hold to me, so handsome as he was, so clever, and with talents far above the ordinary young gentleman of the time?

'It is all very fine for you to jest, Betty. It is no jesting matter to me, child! Have you not known—have you not seen how, from that day when I found you crying on your father's grave, I have loved you?'

I cannot tell what answer I might have given, had not Tommy, with a loud whoop, come tearing into the garden, shouting,—

'Here's Ted! Here's Ted courting Bet!'

'Hold your tongue, you young rascal!' Edmund said, and I sprang to my feet to hear my step-mother say in no very pleased tones,—

'What brings you here, Edmund? I thought you were still at Cambridge?'

'I am on my way to Eastham, five miles off. I turned in here to see you, but I'll put up at the hostel in the village, if so it pleases you, Aunt Anne.'

'Nay, Edmund, be not so testy. You are welcome. Your chamber here is always at your service. Come into the parlour. I'll send the children to bed, and then I'll hear your news.'

It was to my stepmother's interest to be civil to Edmund Pelham. He had a small fortune inherited from his mother, and I had reason to know, in later times, that he had often given a dole of money to his aunt, who was in good sooth only his aunt by marriage, her first husband's sister having married his father, who had made some money as a jeweller and goldsmith in the city.

The last of all familiar things is ever painful. Thus I felt sorrowful when I thought I should never sleep again in the little garret where I had passed many a solitary hour.

The old pear tree, which covered the wall of the house under my lattice, was putting forth its rounded white blossoms, one branch lying across the lower pane of my window.

I leaned out to breathe the fresh, crisp air of the spring night, and looked up at the starlit sky, questioning, as I had often done before, what lay in those depths, concealed by the glare of the sun, and revealed when darkness crept over the face of the earth.

It was but natural that, in the stillness of the night, I should rehearse the words of love Edmund had spoken—natural that it was sweet to me to think there was one who loved me best.

'Not bound,' he said. 'Not bound by any promise.' That cut two ways. If I was not bound, neither was he, and I felt it was but likely he would soon forget me. Yet I would fain believe he would remember, and for myself—ah! for myself—there could never be a doubt. Having learned that I loved Edmund Pelham, I could not forget the lesson henceforth, so I thought!

My farewells were soon spoken the next morning.

My stepmother did not show any regret at my departure. It was a relief to her, and she did not hide it.

Madge and Tommy made me promise I would bring plenty of hardbake and ginger nuts when I came back from London, and Giles and Rhoda— the man and his wife who helped on the farm and in the house—seemed more sorry to lose me than

I could have expected, Rhoda throwing her apron over her head as she turned away from the door to hide her tears, while Giles shouldered my box and I carried the package which held my extra aprons and little matters that did not fit into the chest.

When we got to the hostel to wait for the stage, I found Edmund Pelham there.

I had not seen him that morning, and thought he had gone early to Eastham.

I affected a lightsome mood, which hid my real feelings, and I did my best to jest and laugh, while I would sooner have cried and sobbed. However, there was not time for many words, for the stage came rumbling up, and I was soon stowed away inside the stage with four other passengers, who had many bundles and packages, so that we were near suffocated for air.

I called to Edmund that I would sooner ride on the roof, but he shook his head,—

'No,' he said, coming close to the narrow window. 'No, you had best stay where you are. There are no women on the roof.' He held my hand till the last moment. Then the horn blew, there was a scraping of the horses' feet, and we jogged off.

My fellow travellers were too much occupied with their own concerns to take heed of me, and I soon fell into a dose and slept for the greater part of

B

the journey—awoke once by the coach getting into a rut and being nearly overturned, and got out with much hallooing and noise; and again, later in the day, by a scare as to gentlemen of the road. They stopped the stage, but finding no likelihood of booty, went off for richer prey.

In the dim, fast-fading light of the spring evening, dazed and weary, I found myself in the courtyard of the inn where the stage stopped, and a deep bass voice cried out,—

'Is a young gentlewoman here named Lockwood? Ha!' Mr Gostling said, 'here you are. I overlooked you in the crowd. Now, then, we will get your baggage carried by a hand porter, and I will take care of you to Westminster. Tired, eh?'

'Yes, sir,' I said, 'and cramped in my feet.'

'Poor little one! I will get you a cup of wine ere we set out on foot to Westminster.'

So we turned into the parlour of the hostel, where Mr Gostling ordered a cup of wine and a platter of cakes, bidding me eat and drink and refresh myself.

This was only one of the many acts of kindness I received at the hands of Mr Gostling. There were several people in the parlour, and I heard Mr Gostling say,—

'Ay, it was a wondrous escape. I only marvel I am alive to tell the tale.'

'His Majesty was in peril also,' one of the questioners said.

'In peril! I tell you it was the narrowest escape king or subject ever had.'

'A warning, methinks, a warning; but, 'twixt you and me, sir, if the lady who gave the yacht her name of Fubbs were at the bottom of the sea, it would be the ill wind which blew good to the country.'

'Hush! hush! man; you forget you are speaking before a favourite of His Majesty's, whose bass voice has brought him not only favour but guineas.'

'In a silver egg—is not that so, Master Gostling?'

'You are full of questions,' Mr Gostling said. 'I am not bound to answer them. Come, child, we must be off, or we shall need to hire a link-boy, the evening is closing in.'

I heard all that passed, but I could not understand aught of it.

'Fubbs.' What a queer, ugly name, I thought. Is anyone called in sober earnest Fubbs?

But remembering that Mr Gostling had not been pleased at being questioned by the men in the parlour of the hostel, I forbore to do so.

I trudged along by his side, while he hummed airs in his deep, yet musical voice, and as I passed through the streets and saw what seemed to me unnumbered houses, I began to realise that I was alone in the great city, and my heart turned to him who had spoken words of love to me the evening before.

Why had I jested and laughed when we parted, while Edmund's face showed signs of strong emotion? What would I not have given now for the clasp of his hand—for the sound of his voice?

With these thoughts I stumbled along. My feet, all unaccustomed to the paving stones of a town, ached with soreness and weariness. And my guide, just in advance, walked on, having hired a link-boy to precede him, the lurid light of his torch scarcely needed in the twilight, which was deepening every moment. At last we came to an open space, and Mr Gostling, turning, said,—

'That is the Abbey before you.'

The Abbey! And almost as he spoke the clock chimed for seven; and above the murmur of the city, the call of the link-boys, the footfalls of passers-by, the bells were like a voice from the dark-blue sky above, against which were the massive walls of Westminster Abbey.

It looked so stupendous to me, so vast, so mysterious, I stood looking up at its dim, dark outline till Mr Gostling said,—

'You'll have time enow to gaze at the Abbey, child, for you will live under its shadow.'

CHAPTER II

A. D. 1684

WE now turned into a square under an archway, and Mr Gostling stopped before the door of a small house, on which he gave a thundering rap with the head of his stick. Dismissing the link-boy with the money he asked for, Mr Gostling, always impatient of delay, knocked again.

Then bolts and bars were withdrawn, and a clear voice, many degrees higher in pitch than Mr Gostling's, said,—

'Who could it be bringing the house about our ears but the Reverend Will Gostling.'

'I've brought the little maiden, as agreed,' Mr Gostling said. 'Step in, child, and show yourself to the chiefest musician in England.'

'So saith the biggest bass voice in England or the world,' Mr Purcell replied, with a laugh.

'Come in, come in, and I will call the mistress
You must need your supper,' Mr Purcell said
kindly, 'after your journey.'

I wanted nothing so much as bed, where I might
hide the tears which I had much ado to keep back.
But now I found myself in a parlour, lighted not
only by the lamp hanging from the oak beam that
crossed the roof, but by two large candles standing
on a desk covered with papers. In another corner
of the parlour, in a recess, was a table with a
basket of needlework, and before it Mrs Purcell
was seated.

'Here, then, Fan, is the little handmaiden you
have desired to ease your burdens, and you must
needs give her a welcome.'

Mrs Purcell looked at me with a pair of bright,
searching eyes, and said,—

'She is very small, Henry. What is her age?'

Then, untying my hood, my hair fell down over
my figure.

'Well, she has a growth of hair, in good sooth.
We must cut off some of these heavy locks,
child.'

'May it please you, madam,' I said, 'I am not a
child. I am sixteen years old, and—and—' My
voice was trembling, and, afraid I would burst out
crying, I stopped short.

'Sixteen! Who could have thought it?' Mr Purcell said; 'but hasten to get us supper, dear wife, and then you shall put the little maid to bed. She has had a long and tiresome journey.'

Mrs Purcell went to do her husband's bidding, and I was left in the parlour with Mr Gostling. Mr Purcell went across the passage to another room, whence came the sound of a harpsichord and viola.

'Music, music, concord of sweet sounds! it is the air you will breathe in this house,' Mr Gostling said, and then he seated himself at a harpsichord and began to sing, from a sheet of music which lay on the desk, the words, 'They that go down to the sea in ships.'

The sound of his voice hushed the music in the other parlour, and Mr Purcell came back with a young man. He was quite young himself, only twenty-five.

'I have only wrote those first bars; before I proceed further, my good friend, you must relate the story once more. You gave me but the outline t'other day. Let us have it before supper. It will pass the time, for my good wife is somewhat tardy in her cooking, and needs help, for she has never been strong for work since the birth and death of our little son.'

They seemed to forget my presence. Now, after

long, long years, I can recall myself as I sat on
the high chair where Mrs Purcell had placed me,
my feet scarce touching the ground, my tangled
locks falling over my figure, the desolation of my
heart unsuspected and uncared for. Yet soon, as
I listened to Mr Gostling's story, I forgot my loneliness and forgot myself in the intense earnestness
with which the tale of deliverance was told, with
scarce repressed emotion. Mr Gostling had what is
well called dramatic power of description.

He brought before us the whole scene of danger
and deliverance, so that his listeners might be said
to live it with him over again.

Mrs Purcell, coming in with flushed cheeks from
the kitchen, paused at the parlour door at a sign
from her husband, fearing lest the narrative should
be in any way interrupted.

As far as I can recall it, Mr Gostling's story shall
be written here.

'You may picture to yourself, good Master Purcell,' he said, 'how flattered I felt when His Majesty
ordered me to make one of a party to sail down the
river and round the Kentish coast in the yacht *Fubbs*.'

'His Majesty knew what good company he would
have with you aboard,' Mr Purcell said; 'but proceed—so much I have heard before.'

'However that may be, we were full of mirth

and jollity at our start. His Majesty was at his
wittiest, and he made much fun out of the name of
his yacht. It is said Her chubby Grace of Portsmouth
was not so well pleased to know the round-bowed
yacht bore the soubriquet which His Majesty gives
her—but that by the way. The Duke of York was
aboard, and when we made the North Foreland, his
eye, well accustomed to watch wind and weather
descried an ominous cloud coming up on the wind.
The Duke gave a warning that it was safer to tack,
if by good luck we could enter the river's mouth
again ; but the King laughed and said he liked a
good tossing, even if he were sick, for it was bound
to be a benefit to his stomach, which had been ill at
ease of late. So, disregarding the Duke's warning,
the yacht rode on right into the teeth of the storm.
Ah ! my friend,' Mr Gostling said, 'many a time
and oft have I chanted the words of which, till that
dread moment, I never knew the meaning—" Verily,
they that go down to the sea in ships see the works
of the Lord, and His wonders in the deep." Ere
we could grasp our danger, ere we could prepare
our souls for the coming death, which seemed inevitable, the stormy wind rose and the great waves
lifted up their voices. We were, in truth, carried
up to the black heavens and down again into the
still blacker abyss yawning below. Verily our soul

melted away for very trouble, and we staggered
about the deck as if drunken.   We were at our
wits' end.   His Majesty did not cry out as many
of the crew did, nor lose his cool bearing, though
his face may have been paler than its wont.   But
words fail me to tell you how the two brothers—the
King and the Duke—worked bravely as common sea-
men and did their utmost to save the lives aboard the
Fubbs.   The Duke of York had a marvellous courage
in a strait like that in which we found ourselves—a
marvellous physical courage ; but, alas ! he has not
the courage which will stand him in good stead if he
comes to the crown—but this by the way.   Let me
tell you, Henry Purcell, that nought will ever wipe
away from my mind the distress and well-nigh
despair which seized me in the midst of those
stormy waves ; the masts creaking, the great waters
rushing over our craft, the wind howling, and the
cry for help rising with it from many of us distraught with fear.'   Mr Gostling paused, and then
added,—

'There, my good friend, take that psalm for
your text, and render it into music with the calm
and peace of the words which follow — "For
He maketh the storm to cease, so that the
waves thereof are still."   Ah, we knew the gladness
which followed when we were brought safely into

the haven. Surely we should never cease to praise the Lord for His goodness.'

Mr Purcell did not speak, and we all obeyed Mrs Purcell's summons to supper. And here my memory of that first evening fails.

I believe I fell from my bench at supper in a swoon, for I recall nothing more till I came to consciousness in a little room at the top of the house in a garret no bigger than my own at the Ivy Farm.

I heard Mrs Purcell say,—

'You are better now, and must drink this nice posset.'

I obeyed, and then slept till the sun was peeping in at the narrow lattice. I heard the Abbey chimes, and from below came the sound of a deep bass voice, while the harpsichord was played to accompany it, and I knew it was Mr Gostling singing the words of the psalm which he had bid Mr Purcell to take for the text of his anthem.

Those first few hours in Westminster were memorable hours to me. It would be hard to express, if I tried to do so, what it was to me to enter the choir of Westminster Abbey for the first time.

I had done my best to learn what duties were expected of me, and I found it pleasant to be instructed in them by the gentle voice of Mrs

Purcell. It was, as Mr Gostling said, music, music everywhere.

'You will like to hear evensong in the Abbey,' Mrs Purcell said. 'You can enter the cloister and so find your way into the choir, and Mr Purcell will be at the organ. I have to spare my strength; with so many household cares, and the assistance I give my husband by making, often many times, new copies of his scores with his corrections.'

'I would fain be of use,' I said, 'nor leave you to go to the Abbey if you need me.'

'Oh, I do not choose to make you my slave, child; to speak the truth, since I lost my babe, my little John Baptiste, I have wanted a friend—a companion —and I think I shall find her in you.'

These words thrilled my heart with gladness.

'I know,' Mrs Purcell said, 'your mother was of gentle birth, and well known to our good Master Gostling. Thus I do not look on you as a servant, but, as I said, a friend.'

Then Mrs Purcell stooped and kissed me, and bid me get my hood and cloak, and she would show me from the doorstep the cloister entrance.

I did as I was bid, and ran with a lighter heart than I had felt for some days to the cloister.

The organ was pealing forth as I went in; a man wearing a black gown and with a silver rod in his hand told me to go back to the nave in a stern voice.

'What do ye mean galloping into the Abbey as if you was mad?'

I did not care. I did not answer. I was as well pleased to be in the nave as in the choir. I knelt down on the stone paving, and was spellbound.

The voices of the choristers, the roll of the organ, the arches springing skyward, overwhelmed me. Let those who come after me, and read my story, bear in mind that I was, for the first time in my short life, under the power—the mysterious power—of music as it ascended to the vaulted roof overhead, to the heights of Heaven.

Bear in mind I had within something which the music called to life, something which had faintly answered to the call of Nature's music, as I had told Mr Gostling—the whispering wind, the rippling water, the song of birds. But now there was melody in my heart, a joy as of a treasure discovered, a sense of oneness with the grandeur and the glory above me and around me.

It was but few words I caught when the voices were in full chorus, but when a boy's voice sounded alone I could distinguish them.

'He hath put down the mighty from their seat, and hath exalted the humble and meek.'

But the bursts of joyful praise in the *Gloria* moved
me, though not by any words, for I but dimly understood them or even heard them.

I knelt on—unconscious of eyes which were upon
me—never moving till the last note of the organ
had died away. Then, looking round, I saw the
few worshippers straggling out of the Abbey—talking, laughing, and with scant reverence for the place.
I must needs follow, and, rising, I saw a lady standing by me.

She was tall, and at a glance I could discern that
she was someone of consequence.

A pair of liquid brown eyes, shaded by thick, curled
lashes, sought mine, and she said,—

'You are, methinks, a stranger here, alone in this
big city.'

'No,' I answered. 'No, madam—that is, I have
come to live with Mistress Purcell.'

'Ah! then you are safe,' the lady said. 'Master
Purcell is my friend. Come to the door with me—
I see the vergers wait to close it—and I will walk
to Dean's Yard with you.'

The lady moved with such wondrous grace, her
footfall scarce heard on the pavement, while my
heavy, country-made shoes clicked and clattered by
her side. At the door a chair waited, with lacqueys in attendance.

THE WEST FRONT OF WESTMINSTER ABBEY, IN THE
SEVENTEENTH CENTURY.

'Follow me,' the lady said, 'to Master Purcell's house. It suits me to walk thither with this young gentlewoman.'

Then two gentlemen with flowing curls and, as it seemed to me, all velvet, satin and lace, came forward, bowing low, their caps, with long feathers falling from them, in their hands.

'Fair lady,' one began, 'permit us to escort you, if indeed you venture to discard your chair.'

The lady curtseyed, and then, with a lofty inclination of her head, said,—

'I thank you, Master Mountfort, for your politeness, but I decline the honour you would do me.'

'Nay, be not so cruel,' the second gentleman said. 'We shall do well to guard you from the too bold gaze of those you may meet. We will take no refusal.'

'Hold! nor pester the fair lady with unwished-for attentions;' and the gentleman the lady had called Mr Mountfort put his arm in that of his companion and drew him away.

We were soon in Dean's Yard, and here we met Mr Purcell with a roll of music under his arm.

'Good even to you, Master Purcell. I found this little maiden kneeling in the Abbey, wrapt around with your music, and I have brought her hither.'

'You are ever thoughtful for others, madam. This young gentlewoman is a *protégée* of our good friend

Master Gostling, and he brought her to our house yester evening. Honour us by coming in, and I will show you a new song I have been writing.'

'Nay,' the lady said, 'I must to my chair now I have seen this child—for, sure, she is but a child—safe in your care. Adieu! adieu!' and smiling on me with enchanting sweetness, the lady stepped into her chair and was soon borne out of sight.

'How beautiful she is!' I said.

'Ay! beautiful and good,' Mr Purcell said. 'She calls you a child; she is scarce more herself. She has not reached her twenty-first year.'

'Is she a very grand lady?' I asked. 'A duchess or princess?'

Mr Purcell laughed.

'She is a queen in her own realm, for she is turning the heads of many in the town. She is Mistress Bracegirdle, the budding actress. You shall see her act, and then you will know what she is.'

A new life now opened for me. I soon found strange things grew familiar, and that I was part and parcel of Mr Purcell's household.

The year of my taking up my abode in Dean's Yard was marked by an event of great moment to the world of music in which I now found myself.

This event was the erecting in the Temple Church of two organs for the choice of the Benchers of the Temple. I was busy at the desk, where I was making a copy of 'Saint Cecilia,' an ode lately composed by my master, when Mr Smith entered the room hurriedly.

'Where is the master, child?' he asked—'Master Purcell. What are you about—eh?'

'I am learning, sir, to copy music for the help of Master Purcell, who is so good as to bear with my errors, and is patient in teaching me.'

'Ah! he is one of the wonders of our time. I am come to tell him that all is ready for the trial of my organ and that of Harris on the morrow. I am not afraid of my triumph, because I know full well that Dr Blow and Master Purcell will bring forth all that is best in my organ, despite the fact that Baptist Draghi will do his utmost for Harris; but he has no quarter tones, and herein lies my advantage. Master Purcell knows what these quarter tones mean.'

If Mr Purcell knew, I did not; and while Mr Smith proceeded to tell of the pains and labour he had used to achieve the result of which he was so proud, I sat with my quill in my hand, listening, but not understanding. Presently Mr Purcell came in, and then the two friends left me to my

C

work, which I followed with all the perseverance
I could summon, but often I was sorely puzzled
how to mark the semiquavers, with their long tails
and small heads, and to copy all the signs aright.

Mrs Purcell was absent on this afternoon, and I
was again interrupted in my work by the entrance
of a young gentlewoman, who threw herself down
on the settle, and said,—

'I've come for another order for the Temple
Church on the morrow. Where is Master Purcell?
I am set on getting there, and my uncle is perverse.
Saith he, "You do not care for music, nor know
one air from another." What does that matter? I
like the fun of a crowd, and there are folks in the
Temple I want to see. Perhaps I should say who
I am. You look dazed, and I fain hope you will
know me next time we meet. Your big eyes have
scanned me pretty closely.' A laugh followed this
speech and I felt the colour rush to my face.
'That blush is becoming. Your cheeks are too
pale, child. Now, you are dying to know who I
can be? I am Adelicia Crespion—at your service
—step-niece of the Chanter, his reverence Stephen
Crespion. He is a monstrous strict personage, and,
I dare to say, he would gladly be rid of me. So
he will be when I marry—and I mean to marry—
only I must get a rich suitor, for I hate mean,

sordid ways. Now, who are you? You look a
prim little thing, and might smarten your dress
with advantage.'

I felt this to be very impertinent, and I said,
with all the dignity I could command, which was
not much,—

'My name is Elizabeth Lockwood, and I have
work to do for Master Purcell, so may it please
you to suffer me to proceed with it.'

Again a rippling laugh.

'You are a little oddity, but I like you. You
make a variety to the dressed-up, painted minxes
who turn up their noses at me. I have no especial
friend in Dean's Yard. I was brought up in a
convent in France, and I have only lately come
to my uncle, Stephen Crespion. My father was
his half-brother, and he has taken pity on me, and
has given me a home. Pity! How I detest pity
—don't you? Is it pity that made Mistress Purcell
take you in?—if so, we are in the same plight
and ought to be friends. Have you a father and
mother?'

'No,' I said shortly.

'An orphan, like me. But I am supposed to be
a Catholic, like my poor mother. To speak the
truth, I am nothing. It's no odds to me what
religion I profess. The old nuns wanted me to

stay in the convent and take the veil. Catch me! I wouldn't be like them for all the world. Poor souls! Shut out of the world for ever—dull old frights! No; they weren't all frights. One was a beauty, with such a story. No one knew what it was but me. If the dear old sisters had known, they would have died of it, I verily believe. There, now I have said enough for one day, but I intend to see you often, whether you like me or not. Heigh-ho! I wish Master Purcell would come.'

'He went out with a gentleman, the gentleman who has built one of the organs for the Temple Church.' How I wished my new acquaintance would depart! So I said, 'Will you please to leave a message with me, and I will deliver it.'

'No, I do not please,' was the reply. 'I can get most things I want, and I'll get leave to sit in a good place at the Temple to-morrow. I'll coax Master Purcell till I get it.'

It amazed me to see, when at last Mr Purcell returned, how Mistress Crespion succeeded in getting her way.

Adelicia Crespion had an attraction for gentlemen that none could deny. She could flatter, and coax, and find favour as a plain, unpretending woman could not. So, when Mr Purcell shook his head, saying,—

'Every place in the church is filled. I doubt, madam, that it is impossible to grant your request.'

'No, no, it is not impossible, dear Master Purcell. You won't deny me the delight of hearing you bring out divine sounds from the organ. You are certain to win the day. My uncle says he is sure of it. I must hear you; I must share your triumph. I will sit—or stand—in the loft. I will not incommode you. I will be as prim and quiet as this child who is watching me with her big eyes. Ah! you can't say me nay. I will be here early, and we will start for the Temple together. Here is dear Mistress Purcell,' Adelicia said, springing to meet her and kissing her on both cheeks. 'I am to hear Master Purcell's triumph to-morrow. He has given me permission to sit in the organ gallery. Isn't it good and charming of him? There, I'll give you another kiss, and you must give it to him. Adieu! adieu! *Au revoir! mille remerciments!*'

'Hold! hold! Mistress Crespion. Stop! I have made no promise,' Mr Purcell cried.

'Oh, yes, you have. Silence means consent,' she said, kissing her hand as she flitted across Dean's Yard to the Chanter's house.

'What a lovely creature she is!' Mr Purcell said.
'It is hard to deny her aught.'

'Nay, I will not call her lovely,' Mrs Purcell said.
'I will allow Mistress Bracegirdle is lovely, but not
Adelicia.'

'Thou art lovelier than either in thy husband's
eyes,' Mr Purcell said, and then, with a kiss, he left
us to repair to the Temple for a last rehearsal.

The trial of the two organs brought together a
vast number of people, and it was indeed impossible,
long before the appointed hour, to find standing-
room, so great was the crowd in the Temple
Church.

Adelicia insisted on joining company with me and
Mrs Purcell, and as we were led through the throng
by one of the choristers from the Abbey, I heard
him say to Mrs Purcell,—

'I have only an order for the placing of two in
the gallery.'

And here Adelicia pushed past me, and so thick
was the crowd that I was separated from my
companions.

I was jostled and crushed, and my hood torn from
my head. I was frightened, and tried to make my
way back and get out of the church.

At last I found refuge on the monument of one of

the knights, and so got out of the press for a few
minutes. Only for a few minutes. I was roughly
pulled from my position, and so was another gentlewoman who had climbed on the crossed legs of the
crusader.

'It is forbidden by the Master to climb on the
monuments. You ought to know better,' said a
rough voice.

At this moment a gentleman came through the
crowd, way being made for him. I was ready to
cry with heat and vexation, especially as, looking
up to the gallery, I saw Adelicia Crespion wield-
ing a large fan, with the self-important air which
seemed to say she had, as usual, got her own way.
Yes, by ousting me, for I knew Mrs Purcell would
have desired me to be near her. This gentleman,
who now came close to me, looking at me, said,—

'I will help you to a seat if you will come with
me,' and taking my hand as he would have taken
the hand of a child, he drew me along with him,
and in a few minutes I found myself above the
crowd on a raised bench by the wall, beneath me
rows of the gentlemen of the Temple, who were
assembled at this trial of the two organs.

When I had recovered myself, and settled my dis-
ordered kerchief and rebellious hair, which would make
my hood fall back, I had time to look round me, and

recognised in the gentleman who had befriended me one of those who had met Mrs Bracegirdle at the Abbey door. He had a most pleasant voice, and he kindly said,—

'You belong to Mistress Purcell's household, I think?'

'Yes, sir; I was separated from her in the crowd, and another has taken my place yonder by her side.'

The gentleman smiled, as, looking up to the gallery, he saw Adelicia fanning herself and coquetting with a gentleman who was leaning over her.

'Ah! I see; it is the niece of the Chanter of the Abbey, a young gentlewoman who thinks first of herself and next of other people. Now,' he said, 'I must leave you here, for a friend yonder is beckoning me to join him. He is one of the umpires who is to decide the question as to which organ is best suited for the church. My name is William Mountfort, and that gentleman who is impatient for me to join him is no less a person than the Lord Chief-Justice Jeffreys. When the affair is over I will return and conduct you to the house of Master Purcell, a man I am proud to call my friend. You are not afraid to be left here?'

I was afraid, but anyhow it was better than being jostled in the crowd, and I was seated next an old gentlewoman, who occupied the second seat on the narrow bench, which only had room for two.

Mr Mountfort leaned over me and said,—

'This young gentlewoman will be glad of your protection, madam, till my return. She has missed her friends in the throng and is alone.'

A grunt and a nod was all the answer vouchsafed, and as Mr Mountfort left us she said, giving me a nudge with her elbow,—

'Don't squeeze me, child. Keep to your own place. My back is fit to break as it is, perched up here, and I am like to swoon with the heat, and mind you don't fidget,' for I was obliged to steady myself by putting the point of my toes against the back of the bench before us, and even then I could hardly keep my balance.

But with the first swell of the organ a hush fell over the assembly, and I became unmindful of my uneasy position, of my disagreeable neighbour, who puffed and grumbled and nudged me continually, with a whispered command to keep my distance. The organ built by Mr Harris was heard first, and murmurs of applause followed each performance of music that had no name for me, but thrilled me to my soul with that nameless power of which I have spoken.

There was a pause between the two performances.

There was a movement amongst the rows of be-wigged heads below me. Many of the Benchers straggled out to stretch their legs and doubtless get refreshment, while my neighbour drank out of a vial something which had a strong smell, and munched a large cake till not a crumb was left. Then she settled herself to a nap, her head bent on her breast, snoring loud and as if she were choking, and making a horrid gurgling in her throat.

When the first notes of the other organ sounded she woke with a start, and her face as red as the turkey's comb in the yard at the farm. I wondered what had brought this fat gentlewoman to hear the music, for I do not think it was anything to her beyond noise. I did not know then, as I know now, that fashion leads the way to performances of music, the theatres, and to other exhibitions. Hundreds of people, whose ears are deaf to the voice of the charmer, will rush in crowds, as on this day, to hear music which is to them nought but sound, stirring within them neither feeling nor delight. The touch of my master, as I now love to call Mr Purcell, brought out the full beauty and capabilities of Mr Smith's organ.

I was, as I have said, ignorant at this time of musical terms, and knew naught of quarter notes or the facilities these gave for modulating into remote keys. Yet I felt there was a difference between the music and harmony brought out by Dr Blow and by Mr Purcell, and that which had preceded it on the other organ.

When all was over, I waited as I had been bid till Mr Mountfort came for me. This gave me time to watch the dispersing crowd.

Many of the gentry and nobility were present, and I saw for the first time the gay dames and attendant cavaliers passing before me.

The ladies amazed me, with their high colour and little black patches cut in varied forms on their chin and cheeks. In my ignorance I thought it strange so many had pimples or scratches to hide, and strange, too, that these town gentlewomen should have such rosy cheeks.

I had to learn that the roses were produced by paint, and the little black patches were put to show off the pearly whiteness of the skin, due to powder.

How ignorant I was! and yet by the reading of Shakespeare's plays and other books, lent to me by Edmund Pelham, I knew full well that the story of love made the sum of life to high and low, rich and poor.

Was it to be the sum of life to me? Edmund

Pelham's words had stirred in me a response to his love, and mine for him fluttered in my breast as a bird flutters in its nest when the first rays of the spring sunshine pierce the branches of the tree where it is built, awakening it to life—yes, and to sing the sweetest song of dawning joy and hope.

I do not think I had cause to sing that song at this time. It was more a consciousness that in a crowd such as that where I had found myself that day, there was one absent, yet present to me, who would have been angry to see me left alone to struggle with roughness and uncivil pushing and jostling, by Adelicia's means. I was too much given to think about myself, and all my longings unsatisfied and hopes unfulfilled. Thus it was good for me that I was now to live with people like Mr and Mrs Purcell, and that service for them became heart service, which I never could have given to the harsh and tyrannical woman who had robbed me first of my father's love and then of my birthright. For Edmund Pelham spoke truly when he said I had more right to the proceeds of Ivy Farm and the savings which my father had left behind him than the children of a former husband of my stepmother.

When the church was nearly cleared and I began

to think Mr Mountfort had forgotten me, I saw him coming towards me with another gentleman.

My stout neighbour on the narrow bench had long since taken her departure, and Mr Mountfort said,—

'I crave pardon for leaving you so long, but I have forgotten everything in listening for the decision of those who are competent to judge which organ is the better. Now, if you please, I will conduct you to Dean's Yard, and as it does not lie far out of his way, my friend, the Judge, will accompany us.'

'No, no, not to Purcell's house, Mountfort. The decision is not yet made, and I shall have madam's beseeching eyes turned on me,' was the answer. 'I am only one of a number, and we shall agree by majority of votes.'

'There is not much doubt which organ gains the palm, or which hand was the most skilled to draw forth the melody.'

'Tut, tut, Mountfort, you must not tempt me to divulge what I think. This child,' turning upon me a pair of the sharpest eyes, which glittered under heavy brows, 'this child has music in her, or I'm mistaken. A pupil of Purcell's, is she?'

'Not at present, but I plead ignorance even of her name,' Mr Mountfort said.

A knight-errant, eh, Mountfort? It suits you

well, whether on the stage or off it. Have a care! have a care! There's a pair of lovely eyes casting a spell over you, or I'm mistaken. Don't blush like a damask rose, child,' the Judge said, turning . sharply on me as he parted from us. 'The eyes I mean are not yours, though, in good sooth, yours are like to work mischief.'

'That is Judge Jeffreys,' Mr Mountfort said; 'a good friend of mine, with more wits in his little finger than most of us have in our whole bodies. He is somewhat pitiless in his judgments of other poor mortals, and makes enemies as well as friends.'

Mr Mountfort left me at the door of Mr Purcell's house, saying he had a rehearsal for that night's play, which must not be neglected.

He made me a low bow, treating me, even me, with as much respect and courtesy as he had treated the beautiful lady at the door of Westminster Abbey.

'William Mountfort, madam, asks by what name he is to remember you.'

'Betty Lockwood, sir, who thanks you for your goodness to her, which she will never forget.'

'A slight service to win me such a meed of praise,' was the answer, as Mr Mountfort turned and left me.

I found Mrs Purcell lying on the settle, propped up by cushions. She looked exhausted, and said,—

'I am thankful you have come, Betty. You must prepare supper and make Henry a pasty—take care not to burn it, and see the sage and onions are chopped fine. All is put ready to your hand. Why did you leave me? I was so weary with Adelicia and her coquetting and folly. You should not have left me.'

'I could not avoid it, madam,' I said, feeling ready to cry. 'I was so pushed and jostled, and—'

'Well, well, go to the kitchen and do your best, and I will try to sleep. We do not know yet which organ will be chosen. Never did Henry play more divinely. His name and fame are dear to me—you will know how dear when you have a husband to be proud of. I heard voices at the door. Who was it?'

'Master Mountfort,' I said, and I felt the hot colour rise to my face.

'Ah! he is a young actor of great promise; he adores Mistress Bracegirdle, and she has many at her feet—some who owe him a grudge for the favour she shows him. I hope no ill will come of it.'

I left Mrs Purcell to do my duty in the kitchen, and having had nothing since I broke my fast, I was very glad to eat a manchet of dry bread and take a sup of beer.

I found myself singing as I worked, chopping the

herbs to the tune of a Toccata of my master's, and catching, it may be, the air imperfectly. Presently Mr Purcell came in.

'Who is that singing the air of my Toccata that I was playing yester evening.? You! little Betty. Why, you must be taught to sing and modulate your voice—find the quarter notes, eh? My wife is weary with this day's work, and troubles herself with fears that Smith's organ will not be chosen. I have no fears, for I know these quarter notes will strike the balance in Smith's favour. If it does, I may chance to get a little of the credit. But what is credit worth, and what is money worth, when compared with the love of music for its own sake? I would gladly eat bread and drink water instead of that pasty you are making with such clever fingers, if the choice were given me between scant food and the power to make music which God has given me. Child! they talk of the music of the spheres and the golden harps of Heaven; I don't doubt those celestial regions are blessed with the sweetest sounds, but it cannot be to the inhabitants of the Heavenly City what it is to us as we tread the thorny paths of this toilsome world. Music is to us the gift of God to raise us upwards, to lighten care, to soften sorrow, to be a balm for the wounds of the spirit which we all have to bear. So, little

Betty, you see that music to us here below must mean more blessedness than to the dwellers in the Golden City of which the Book of the Revelation tells.'

As my master spoke, his face was illumined and beautiful to behold, as with the ecstasy of a lover who was extolling the charms of his mistress.

Now, after the lapse of many a long year, I can see my master, Henry Purcell, as I saw him then— and such a face, glowing with the light from within, I never saw, nor ever shall see again.

Then, as if coming back to earth, he said gaily,—

'I will go and do my best with the "Welcome Song" for the King's return. I do not feel inspired with Tom Flatman's words, but he is amazingly pleased with them, so I must render them, and then be ready for "the serene and rapturous joys" which I shall know when I eat that pasty made by your hands, little Betty.'

'From these serene and rapturous joys' was the first line of the ode written to welcome back the King to Whitehall.

How little did we think it would be His Majesty's last return to his palace.

I cannot find that anything else worthy of note happened this year which would please those who read my story if I recorded it.

D

I grew daily more satisfied with my new home, for home it was to me.

For the first time in my life I tasted the sweetness of being of use and, I may say, loved and valued for my poor services.

Mrs Purcell was weak and unable to exert herself in matters about the house. Thus, I could spare her exertion, and I grew daily more attached to her and the dear master.

If from ill-health Mrs Purcell was a little disposed to be fractious and complaining, and would give me a few 'quips and quirks,' and speak crossly to me, I did not heed it, for I knew it was but the passing temper of a moment, and that she really loved me.

The visits of Adelicia Crespion were frequent, and she had the power when with me of making me forget her faults, and that she was, as was proved, untrustworthy. But she kissed me, and swore eternal friendship and—this might be a benefit to me—undertook to transform me, as she said, from a country to a town mouse.

I found I was vain enough to be pleased with my new cap, made from my mother's old lace, which also bordered an apron and kerchief for best wear, garnished with a quantity of blue ribands Adelicia had cast off.

Then the old brocade and taffeta, which had belonged to my mother, were renovated, and my hair — that rebellious hair — taught by Adelicia's dainty fingers, with pins and combs, to keep itself within bounds under the coif of blue riband which she made for me.

My black hood was lined with a bright bit of cherry-coloured sarcenet, and I was quite pleased to see how well it became me.

I even wished Edmund could see me, but I had no word or sign from him all through the year. Adelicia did her best to win my love, and Mrs Purcell startled me one day by saying she wondered what Adelicia wished to gain by all her attentions to me.

'There is nought to gain from me,' I said. But Mrs Purcell shook her head and said she was not so sure, adding,—

'I cannot help myself. I love Adelicia when I am with her; but, Betty, I never trust her.'

BOOK II

1685—1686

Love all ; trust a few ;
Do wrong to none ; be able for thine enemy
Rather in power than use, and keep thy friend
Under thy own life's key.
SHAKESPEARE,
All's Well that Ends Well—Act I.

CHAPTER III

A.D. 1685

THIS year opened with a frost so bitter that the sufferings of the poor were very great.

The River Thames was frozen for a few days; then there was a thaw, which was unwholesome by reason of the damp and mire and mud, which made the streets well-nigh impassable, and the constant drip, drip from the eaves, with the dark sky overhead, caused much depression of spirit and sickness.

I felt this the more as Mrs Purcell was much affected by the damp, and seemed unable to forget herself and her ailments.

The master was too much engrossed with his beloved music to yield to low spirits. It was to him, as he said, the very joy and comfort of his life.

Never a day passed but I was permitted by Mrs Purcell to go to evensong in the Abbey, and with my thick pattens, which lifted me out of the mire,

I used to cross Dean's Yard to the cloisters as if on wings, rather than with the slow progress with clogged feet.

Well do I recall the February afternoon, when the lengthening days gave hope of spring, despite the dull thaw, which seemed as if it would never clear away the masses of frozen snow or melt the ice lying in broken blocks on the river.

Adelicia Crespion did not care to expose herself to the bad weather, for it did not suit her complexion, and made the ribands on her hood hang limp and damp.

But this afternoon she overtook me, saying,—

'I am in a religious fit, little Betty, so I am coming to the service. It is so abominably dull yonder. My uncle is as cross as two sticks.'

She put her hand, as was her wont, caressingly into my arm, and we went to our seats in the choir, for no verger could interfere with the Chanter's niece.

By this time I had learned to know the Abbey well. Every spare moment I would go and prowl about, and delight my eyes with the delicate beauty of Henry the Seventh's Chapel, and read on the tombs of many great ones who lie under the shadow of the mighty Minster the story of their lives—'So soon passeth it away, and we are gone, this transitory life of ours.'

These words were ofttimes in my mind, and
more especially to-day, for the Chanter prayed for
our Sovereign Lord the King, who lay in extreme
sickness, and who was in sore need of the fervent
prayers of his people.

Beautiful exceedingly was the music, which
made every verse of the psalms full of meaning,
so wondrous was the master power to wed the
music to the words. How the organ pealed forth
at 'The voice of the Lord shaketh the wilderness;
yea, the Lord shaketh the wilderness of Kadesh!'

Then, as a message from the heavens, came
the soft sweetness of the closing words of hope
and promise—'The Lord shall give His people the
blessing of peace.'

As we rose to leave the Abbey, a faint ray of
sunshine came straggling in at the big west window, and fell upon the figure of a gentleman
standing just where it made a pathway of light.
My heart beat so fast that I could almost hear
its throbs, for the man was Edmund Pelham.

'Betty!' he exclaimed, and then we clasped
hands, forgetting everything but the presence
of each other till reminded by a laugh from
Adelicia.

'So the suitor has come at last!' she said in an
undertone, but it reached Edmund's ears.

When we were outside the Abbey, Adelicia, I saw, took in at a glance that it was worth playing off her airs and graces upon Edmund. She began forthwith to do so, casting admiring glances upon him with her large, lustrous eyes, which, she always persuaded herself, were equal to those of Mrs Bracegirdle, though, indeed, she was in this greatly mistaken, for, if lustrous, they had none of the enchanting softness of Mrs Bracegirdle's.

I was dumb with heart-joy at the appearance of Edmund, for it is ever so with me when deeply moved. I am silent—words will not come at my bidding. They came fast enough whenever Adelicia pleased—and very soon, before we had reached Mr Purcell's door, she was chattering to Edmund as if she had known him for years.

And he seemed amused and pleased with her, though now and again he looked down at me as if inviting me to join in the talk. But Adelicia's attention was now diverted by a smart gallant coming up to her with a low bow. I recognised him as one of the gentlemen who had asked to escort Mrs Bracegirdle to Dean's Yard on the day I first saw her at the Abbey. If ever a man had an evil face, this man had one. But Adelicia flushed crimson, and was apparently pleased to see him.

NORTH TRANSEPT OF WESTMINSTER ABBEY, IN THE
SEVENTEENTH CENTURY.

'I have been to the Chanter's house, madam,' he
said, 'with a missive from Mistress Bracegirdle, who
would fain have your presence at the theatre to-
night, where she is acting Portia in "The Merchant
of Venice"—the first time she has undertaken so
prominent a part; but I swear she will be such a
lovely Portia as was never seen on the boards yet.'

Adelicia pouted, and said,—

'I thank you, Captain Hill, for your obliging offer,
but I know my good uncle would as soon see me
dead as at the play to-night.'

'What a cruel disappointment!' Captain Hill said,
leering at me in an odious fashion, which made
Edmund say sharply,—

'We cannot stand parleying in the cold any
longer. May I enter Master Purcell's house with
you, Betty?'

I lifted the latch of the door, and we passed in
together, leaving Adelicia outside.

To my surprise she called out,—

'May I not come in also?' and turning to Captain
Hill she said, 'Make my respectful compliments and
thanks to Madam Bracegirdle, and say I regret not
seeing the loveliest Portia who was ever on the
boards.' Then, with a toss of her head, she followed
us into the parlour.

I was greatly chagrined at her forcing herself

upon us—I had so much to hear from Edmund—
and it is a marvel that Adelicia did not discover
she was not wanted. But I verily believe she was
so vain that she thought there could not be a
moment when her presence was not a boon in any
company. She threw back her warm hood and
cloak, seated herself on the settle, stretched out
her small, well-shod feet to the blaze of the fire, on
which a fresh log had lately been put, and seemed
perfectly at her ease.

It was necessary for me to seek Mrs Purcell, and
ask her permission to bid Edmund to stay to
supper.

'Who is he?' she asked.

'He is a relation of my stepmother, and—'

'Bid him stay by all means, Betty; but you
must prepare the supper. I am too sick to give
any assistance. Who is below?'

'Adelicia Crespion. She came in unasked,' I
said.

'She ever deems her company is desired; but she
must not be affronted; she is the Chanter's niece,
and Henry is careful to keep in the good graces of
the Chapter of the Abbey.'

Adelicia seemed in fine spirits when at last, after
preparing the supper, I was free to return to the
parlour. And Edmund also looked well pleased

with his company. A pang of jealousy shot through my heart, and, I doubt not, my face told its tale.

Edmund rose when I said supper was served, and we went to the other parlour where it was laid out.

Presently Mr Purcell came in.

'There is bad news of His Majesty,' he said; 'the physicians do not think he will live through the night. There are prayers offered in the Court chapels, the chaplains taking it in turn every quarter of an hour. There is great trouble in the palace, and fears that the King is desiring the popish offices, for he rejects the Holy Communion administered by the Bishop of Bath and Wells. There are dark days coming, I fear me, for the Church and Kingdom.'

A loud rapping at the door made us all start, and, Mr Purcell hastening to open it, we heard a voice ask,—

'Is Mistress Crespion here?'

'My uncle!' Adelicia exclaimed. 'Now pity me, all of you; I shall be scolded like a naughty child.'

'Bid her come without delay,' we heard the Chanter say. 'No, no, Master Purcell, I cannot suffer my niece to absent herself from my house for hours with never a word of apology. No, no, I will await her coming here.'

'You would not have me, Uncle Stephen, come bareheaded into the cold night? I must needs don my cloak and hood.'

This was spoken in loud, shrill tones. Then she put her arms round me, and kissed me again and again, saying,—

'Sweet Betty, adieu! adieu!' Then a curtsey, with a bewitching smile to Edmund, and she was gone.

We supped together, Mr Purcell, Edmund and I, for I carried up Mrs Purcell's supper, as she felt too sick to come down to the parlour.

Then, while Edmund and Mr Purcell talked, I listened.

I had never seen Edmund so agreeable, and I could but admire the way in which he entered into Mr Purcell's favourite topic, and begged that he might hear him play his last new piece for the harpsichord.

He was just about to gratify him when he was summoned by one of the choristers of the Chapel Royal to attend a practice of an anthem in the other parlour. Then Edmund and I were left alone.

'Did you think I was faithless, Betty? How many months is it since we parted?'

'Near a year,' I said.

'And you are glad to see me, Betty?'

My eyes filled with tears. How could he ask such a question?

'Well,' he said, 'I have done with stuffing a dunderhead with Greek and Latin, and I am come to take up my chambers at the Temple to study law in good earnest. So you will often see me, and we shall be happy. Is it so, Betty?'

'Yes,' I said, but my heart told me there was a change since the evening in the porch of Ivy Farm when he told of his love. A change—and what was it?

He looked handsomer than ever. He was noble in appearance, and I felt proud of him—proud that he could care for me.

'Now tell me what you have done here. Are you well treated? Are these people good to you?'

'So good that I love them,' I said; 'and then I have the Abbey near me, and music—such music!'

'A dreamy little maiden as ever, I see,' Edmund said. 'Are the books shut now music has the first place?'

'No; I read my Shakespeare and Spenser, and Stella and Astrophel; but I have learned to think the Bible the best book, and the grandest poetry is to be found in it, surely.'

'Turned Puritan—is that it?' Edmund asked, pinching my ear and then kissing it. Do not

turn Puritan for my sake, child.' Then with a
laugh, 'Your friend with the bright eyes is no
Puritan. What is her name? What kisses she
gave you at parting. I see you are like lovers.'

'No,' I said; 'you mistake. I like Adelicia well
enow, but I do not love her.'

'And do you say the same of me? You like me
well enow, but you do not love me.'

'You know it is not so,' I replied, drawing away
from him.

'Forsooth, I do not know,' he said; 'that farewell of yours at the door of the stage wagon was
cold enow, and you were blithe while I was
sad.'

I could not reply to this. My heart was sore to
think how little Edmund understood me.

'Well, I must take my leave now. I need not
wait to see Master Purcell. You must make my
adieux for me. What a voice that is,' he exclaimed,
as Mr Gostling, who was rehearsing an anthem,
made the house almost shake with his bass voice,
followed by an angelic treble of one of the chief
choristers of the Chapel Royal.

Then Edmund took my hand in his, drew me
towards him, kissed me lightly on the forehead,
and left me.

A sense of unsatisfied longing oppressed me. For

all he said, for all he did, I felt there was a change
—or had I changed? What was it?

The next morning the news of the King's death
was sent by special messenger to the Dean, and
Mr Purcell was summoned to consult as to the
funeral anthem and other music which was to be
sung in the Abbey.

Orders were given that the King should be buried
in a vault beneath the beautiful Chapel of King
Henry the Seventh, and there, without any pomp
or ceremony, he was laid to rest.

Everyone wore black, and there was a general
feeling of solemnity and mourning which affected
all, however humble or however great.

How quick was the change from mourning to
rejoicing! In our little household nothing was
talked of but the coming Coronation of the new King.

Mr Purcell was at work all day, superintending
the building of an organ behind the seats of the
King's Choir of Vocal Music, who were to sit in a
gallery under one of the south arches of the chancel.

He scarce gave himself time to snatch any food,
and he was busy often till the morning hours with
the composition of two anthems for the Coronation.
These anthems were thought very beautiful, and they
received the unstinted praise of all who heard
them.

E

There would be a vast crowd in the Abbey on the 23d of April, and it was doubtful if any place could be obtained for Mrs Purcell.

Mr Purcell was teased and troubled by the clamour of people begging him to favour them by getting them seats, or even room to stand. So benign and kindly was Mr Purcell's nature that it was rare indeed to see him moved to irritation or anger, but he lost patience with those who besieged his door and prayed him to get them admission to the Abbey.

'I tell you,' he said, pushing his way through the throng of supplicants; 'I tell you I can scarce promise my wife that she shall see the Coronation, and is it possible that I can give you admission? Do not press me unduly, madam,' he said to one persisting gentlewoman, 'and be gone.'

This happened on the day before the Coronation, and I grieved to see how weary the dear master was when, that evening, he threw himself down on the settle, and sighed out,—

'"Oh that I had the wings of a dove, then would I flee away and be at rest." Here Frances,' he said, calling Mrs Purcell to him; 'here is a purse full of gold for you; they have paid me for my services in supervising the building of the little organ.'

Mrs Purcell's eyes brightened.

'The money is very welcome, dear heart,' she said, 'though your services cannot be paid for with gold.'

'I must give our good child Betty some of the spoil,' Mr Purcell said, and putting his hand in the bag he bid Mrs Purcell hand me two gold pieces. 'Well earned! well earned!' the dear master said, 'for the dozen of copies you have made of the score of my anthem, "I was glad when they said unto me."'

I knelt and kissed his hand, and said I needed no reward for what I did. Did not he and Mrs Purcell give me a home and treat me with kindness such as I had never known before?'

Then Mrs Purcell kissed and embraced me, and said she hoped I would always find my home with them.

'No! no!' Mr Purcell said; 'not always. Betty will have a home of her own when that young gentleman of the Bar has made his way upward, as he surely will.'

Everyone was astir at dawn the next morning. The ladies of the Court and the wives and daughters of the nobility were dressed over-night for the great occasion.

I watched from my window in the roof those fine ladies thronging the entrance to the Abbey by the cloisters, but the great crowd was collected in the square before the big west door.

I was left in charge of the house, and was well content not to risk being jostled and pushed about as I had been in the Temple Church.

When the Abbey clock struck six, the doors were opened, and the rush which I saw from my little window was very great.

Those set to watch the doors had much ado to prevent these eager folks from being crushed to death, and presently I saw two men bearing out of the crowd a gentlewoman who had swooned.

Soon there was a loud knocking at the door, which had been bolted and barred, and I hastened downstairs to open it.

Mr Mountfort was standing there, and cried in a voice of distress,—

'This is Master Purcell's house. Ah! and I know you, madam. I pray you let us bring in Mistress Bracegirdle, who has swooned in the unmannerly crowd by the cloister door.'

He did not wait for an answer, but rushed back meeting two men, who were bearing Mrs Bracegirdle in their arms. One of these men was Edmund Pelham, the other that evil-faced man they called Captain Hill. He strode in with his burden, and laid her on the settle. Her beautiful hair had fallen from her hood, and lay in rich masses over her shoulders.

'Hasten and fetch water,' Captain Hill said, 'and a burnt feather and vinegar.'

I did not like the peremptory order given me, though I was pleased to have the chance of serving Mrs Bracegirdle.

Mr Mountfort spoke after a very different fashion, and said,—

'Mistress Lockwood will do her best to get what is needful; she is the friend, not the serving-maid in this house.'

But Edmund Pelham had gone to the kitchen before I could reach it, and gave me a cup of water from a pail standing there.

'Where is the vinegar?' he asked.

'I will find it and a feather, for we plucked a capon yesterday; but do you hasten with the water.'

'That villain Hill needs a horsewhip for daring to address you as he did,' Edmund said, as he went off with the water.

'Oh, do not quarrel with that man,' I cried, 'he looks so wicked.'

'And his looks do not belie him,' was the reply.

I soon filled a mug with vinegar, and held the capon's feather—which I had put in a locker the day before—to the smouldering fire on the hearth. It was all done more quickly than I can tell it,

and when I returned to the parlour Mrs Bracegirdle had been sprinkled with the water, and had
opened her beauteous eyes.

'I am not wont to swoon,' she said, with a faint
smile, 'except on the stage, where they tell me I
feign it well. I know not how this came about.
Thanks to you, my good, kind friend,' Mrs Bracegirdle said, putting out her hand to Mr Mountfort,
'I am safe out of that unruly throng.'

'Nay, fair lady,' Captain Hill said, 'you do me
wrong—it may not please you to hear it—but it was
my happy fortune to bear you in my arms to this
place of refuge, with the help of this gallant gentleman of the law. Mountfort may die of the green-
eyed monster if he likes—I see it peeping out of
his eyes even now.'

'Have a care sir! have a care!' Mr Mountfort
said. 'I will brook none of your insults.'

'Nor will I brook any quarrelling,' Mrs Bracegirdle
said, raising herself into a sitting posture. 'For
shame, gentlemen!' as Captain Hill put his hand on
his sword-hilt. 'I am about to ask a favour of you
both—of you all,' she said, turning to Edmund.
'Leave me, I pray you, here under the care of this
sweet child, and should I dare to encounter it, I
will make another effort to enter the Abbey. Now,'
she said imperiously, 'do as I bid you, Captain Hill.

And you,' she said to Mr Mountfort, in a voice of gentle entreaty, 'you will not need a second bidding; you are ever kind and considerate.'

'Methinks, though it may be I say this now in the light of subsequent events, which are now in the far distant past—methinks Mrs Bracegirdle did unadvisedly to rouse the vindictive jealousy of Captain Hill. It smouldered long after this scene in Mr Purcell's parlour, but it never died out, and only gathered strength as do the volcanic fires of which we read, that bide their time to burst forth with fury.

Mr Mountfort bent on one knee and kissed the hand held out to him, while Captain Hill turned on his heel, and, with a discordant laugh, said to Edmund,—

'Come, Pelham, let us be off like whipped curs, with our tails between our legs ; but curs can show their teeth and bite too when their blood is up.'

'We will follow you,' Edmund said, to my great satisfaction, for I could not bear the thought of any friendship between him and this man. 'I will wait to see Mistress Bracegirdle quite restored.'

'We will return,' Edmund said, as he left the parlour with Mr Mountfort, who turned to look back with sad, regretful eyes at Mrs Bracegirdle. 'I will return —it is yet scarcely past seven—and I may chance even now to obtain for you and Mrs Bracegirdle a place where you may witness this ceremony. Adieu, Betty!'

When they were gone, to my great surprise, Mrs Bracegirdle burst into tears.

'Oh, child,' she said, 'may you never know the cruel fate of an actress!'

'Cruel!' I said. 'It seems to me, dear madam, that you are to be envied.'

'Envied? Ah! you do not understand. My fervent prayer is to be kept as pure as when I was a little child playing in the cowslip fields in Surrey. But it is useless to blind one's eyes to the truth. A woman who earns her bread on the stage is surrounded with temptations; and, with all morality set at nought at the Court, is it to be wondered at that, in a company of men and women who are brought together by a common interest, they should sometimes turn the similitude of love which they show to one another every night on the boards into the reality? This is a curse —yes, a curse,' she repeated, 'to a woman who is the fashion for beauty and acting; for, mind you, there is fashion in this—a following where others lead. Have you not seen one goose stretch her wings and waddle across a common, when others, who have been content to squat in a pleasant spot, must needs all run after their leader, cackling as they go, often to find they had better have stayed where they were, for they have perchance run into danger of being scattered by a shepherd's dog or some other enemy? Ah, yes! there is a fashion which sways men and women as well as geese ; where one who is thought a good judge goes, others must needs follow. Poor fools ! poor fools ! and poor women who are pursued by them ! But '—changing her mood, and her eyes lighted up with the marvellous lustre which none who saw can forget—'but I love to be Portia, and I *am* Portia for the time, and then I feel transported above mean and sordid surroundings to all that is noble and good. And yet, child, we can spare pity for the ignoble, as I do for the old Jew. Yes, I pity him—I pity him as he totters away burdened with his weight of years and weight of wickedness and saith, " I am not well." I feel my eyes fill with tears, though I have saved Antonio and effected his ruin. Poor Shylock—poor those who are like him and vindictive and base. These need our pity, ay, our tears, more—far more—than the pure and the up-right and the honourable.'

I was so enthralled by Mrs Bracegirdle's talk, so enchanted by her beauty, that I forgot everything in the pride I felt of being admitted to her con-fidence. I forgot the magnificent scene which everyone was all agog to witness. I forgot the lurking disappointment I had felt when left alone that morning; surely I had no cause to regret it now, now that I had this beautiful lady talking to me as a friend.

She asked me to restore her hair to order, adding, with a smile,—

'You, too, are troubled with a weight of hair, and may well manage mine.'

While I did her bidding, she told me of her friendship with Mr Mountfort, of his marvellous gifts of mimicry, of his intimacy with the Chief Justice Jeffreys.

'Opposites often find pleasure in each other's society,' she said ; 'it is the case here, for sure no two men were to all seeming so different as the Judge and William Mountfort. Not a month ago, at an entertainment of the Lord Mayor and Aldermen, the Judge, being a guest, called Will Mountfort to plead a feigned cause, in which he mimicked some gentleman of the Bar and judges on the bench with such wit and humour that the company were fit to die of laughing. With all his gifts he is ever modest, and has no arrogant manners like so many I could name. He is my friend, and I am proud to own it. I am longing for him to wed with the daughter of a friend of mine, also an actor, Mistress Susanna Perceval. She is worthy of his love; and as to

him, he is worthy of the best woman that is to be
found on earth.'

I had just completed Mrs Bracegirdle's toilette,
and had brought some wine and cake for her refreshment from our little store in the buttery, when
there was again loud knocking at the door.

I was hastening to open it, when Mrs Bracegirdle
said,—

'Hold! Have a care whom you admit; inquire
who goes there ere you open the door.'

I had not need to hesitate long. I heard Adelicia's
voice,—

'Open, open the door, Betty—here is news for you.

Then as I obeyed she rushed in to say her uncle,
Mr Crespion, had a seat for me with her to see
the Coronation, and I must come at once—he was
waiting at the cloister door.

'I cannot come in this guise,' I said; 'it is not
possible,' for I was in my short home-spun skirt
and bodice, with only a thick linen kerchief, and
no cap.

'You shall come! you must come! it is a shame
Mr Purcell has left you behind.'

Adelicia was so intent on her errand that she
had not noticed Mrs Bracegirdle's presence.

'Make her get ready, madam,' she said, appeal-
ing to her.

And Edmund now appeared, according to promise, to conduct Mrs Bracegirdle back to the Abbey.

'Take my place,' I said to Mrs Bracegirdle;
'it must be a good place — and I would sooner
stay at home I could not make myself ready in
time. I could not. Do not urge me.'

I thought if Edmund had added his entreaties
to Adelicia's I might have complied, but he said,—

'It may be as well, for if we delay, our chance of
getting into the Abbey will be small.'

Mrs Bracegirdle did not, I saw, wish to leave
me, but Adelicia clamoured for haste and Edmund
again repeated,—

'It may be as well, but do not delay.'

So in another moment I was alone. I locked
and barred the door, and then, I scarce knew why,
I flung myself on the settle where Mrs Bracegirdle
had rested, and cried bitterly.

It was not altogether, no, not at all, from disappointment about the Coronation. It was from
the feeling, growing stronger and stronger, sorer
and sorer as time passed, that Edmund Pelham's
love for me had waned. Had he not on that
spring evening a year ago pressed his love on me,
though declaring he would not bind me by any
promise—neither was I bound. Ah, me! at seventeen a maiden scarce knows her own heart, for it

The Coronation of James II. and Mary of Modena.

is stirred by the first breath of love and deems that to be eternal which is maybe, like all earthly things, to prove fleeting and transitory.

I felt then, and I know now, that I had not shown Edmund what was indeed in my heart. I cannot tell how it is or why; but I know now, that, if I wished, as I did wish, to keep him true to me, I should have spoken and acted differently towards him, and perhaps—

But what avails it to be mourning over a dead past—a dead love. Yet, even now, as I stand by its grave, I am filled with sadness, and a strange longing for that which then seemed lost to me for ever.

The huzzas of a thousand voices reached my ears as the people hailed the King and his Queen on their coming to the great west door of the Abbey.

The bells rang a joyous peal, and the swell of the organ reached me, with the faint sound of the voices of the choristers, as I sat by the open lattice of my chamber in the roof.

It was a long-drawn-out ceremony, and lasted for hours.

It was near five o'clock, when the sun of the April day was nearing the west, and gleamed on every pinnacle of the Abbey and roofs of the houses clustering round it, that I saw Mrs Purcell and the dear master making their way through the crowd in Dean's Yard towards their home.

I ran down to meet them joyfully, for I was weary of my loneliness and my own thoughts.

Mrs Purcell was faint and tired, and I was glad I had prepared refreshment for her.

'I would you had heard Henry's anthem; it was grand, and beautiful beyond anything you can imagine.'

'Now, dear wife, moderate your praise. I shall do better yet. The anthem owed much to the voices which rendered it. The basses were wondrously true, and it was verily a volume of sound which rose and fell with grandeur and pathos. I can take small praise for that.'

'You take praise for nought you do,' Mrs Purcell said. 'No one values you so little as you value yourself.'

'And if it is so, I am on the safe side, dear heart, but only those who have music in their souls know how the expression thereof falls far, far short of that to which they would fain give utterance.'

'The acclamations for the King and Queen were not as hearty as I expected,' Mrs Purcell said.

'No, there is a whisper of discontent on the

score of religion. The omission of the administration of the Sacrament after the anointing and crowning of the King and Queen could not find favour.'

I asked why it had not been administered.

'Do you not know, child,' my master said, 'that both King and Queen are Roman Catholics—papists is a better word. There is dissatisfaction in the King setting up the crucifix, and having celebrations of the Mass in his private chapel. He will have need of all his wisdom to keep clear of the quicksands around him. He has a splendid presence and a courtly manner, with more dignity than his late majesty ever showed. The Queen's face is very fair, and I can never forget her serious demeanour, raising her eyes to Heaven and apparently wrapt in devotion rather than thinking of the splendour of the robes with which she was clothed and the jewelled crown set on her head. A gentleman about Court told me that the change in manners there is much for the better. Sunday evening acting, with gaming and profaneness, is stopped; and the Duchess of Portsmouth—she who gave the name of "Fubbs" to the yacht in which all aboard nearly lost their lives—has been made aware she must keep her distance from the Queen. But I must away to my work; I am getting through an ode in honour of the King, which

asks, "Why are all the Muses mute?" I must tune
my lyre and wake it to some purpose. But it is but
yesterday my ode to welcome King Charles to
Whitehall was sounding in this house as I played
it for you to hear, my Frances. Poor King! he has
left behind him sore hearts, for, with all his faults,
he was winsome to those he favoured. Master
Gostling is one—and here he comes to tell you as
much.'

'Ay,' Mr Gostling said, throwing himself down on
a vacant chair. 'Ay, I have lost a good friend in
King Charles—always in a merry mood and full of
jests. He called me his gosling, whose deep-toned
voice he preferred to that of the shrill nightingale.
I have the silver egg the King gave me full of
guineas, to keep him and his gracious kindness to
me ever in remembrance. Not the guineas—they
have gone the way of all my money, which burns
in my pocket till it is spent. I must always grieve
that His Majesty never lived to hear the anthem
which commemorates our deliverance. Let us have
it now, my good friend, and it will please me to
think how it would have pleased him for whom it
was written.'

'No, no! not to-night, Gostling. Come with me
and hear what you can say in praise of my new
ode.'

'A new ode for a new king! Ay! well-a-day, so goes this changing world. But mark me, Purcell, you will have to write more odes in praise of yet newer kings ere many years—it may be months—have rolled over your head.'

'You are always given to prophecy,' Mr Purcell said, 'and your prophecies don't often come true. So away with foreboding of evil.'

'Let me give you an air on my viol di gamba which came into my head as I watched that grand procession file into the Abbey this morning.'

'No. To say the truth, I wish that vile instrument of yours had gone to the bottom of the sea when the waves swept so much off the *Fubbs* in the storm.'

'A cruel wish,' Mr Gostling said, laughing, 'but happily unfulfilled;' and forthwith he took the despised instrument in his hand and began to play on it.

Mr Purcell put his fingers in his ears and rushed into the other parlour, saying,—

'It maddens me to hear that ziegle, ziegle, zieg. With a voice like yours, Gostling, I marvel that you can endure to make a noise like the screeching of owls or the discordant caw of rooks and crows.'

Mr Gostling only laughed, and went through the air as if nothing had been said.

F

And with the zieg, zieg, zieg ringing in my ears, I went to prepare a warm posset for Mrs Purcell, before I went to my own chamber to sleep soundly after the long day—the day of King James's Coronation.

CHAPTER IV

A. D. 1686

THERE was for me, who had never known the sweetness of family ties, a great charm in sharing in the
joys and sorrows of those who had given me a home.

As I look back on those years, I feel that the
great events then startling the world did less affect
me than the joy—soon turned to sorrow—of the
birth and death of my dear master's little son
Thomas, who stayed but a few short days with
us, and was laid in his grave in the cloisters of
the Abbey.

This was the second trial which had been sent
my good friends to bear; for before I took up my
abode in Dean's Yard, a little son, baptised John
Baptiste, had been born and died.

These losses of her infants affected Mrs Purcell's
health, and she was scarce able to rouse herself
even to take pleasure in Mr Purcell's increasing
fame.

She would weep bitterly at times, and almost

grudge to see her husband entering with zest into his compositions, which followed each other in marvellous quick succession.

It was in vain old Mrs Purcell remonstrated with her daughter-in-law, and, perhaps, too sharply at times. It was in vain that Mr Purcell's young brother Daniel came to be congratulated on his election to the post of organist at Magdalen College, Oxford.

Mrs Purcell could not rejoice with those who rejoiced, and I saw the disappointment she caused day after day.

'Only a babe of a few days old. How can anyone mourn for him?'

Such was the question Mr Daniel Purcell asked me when he came down from a visit to his sister in her own chamber.

'It is a real grief and sorrow to her,' I said.

'Pshaw! she ought not to sit and mope and cry; she ought to think of other folks. Our good mother loses all patience with her.'

'But her husband does not,' I said. 'He is sorely stricken also, but has his music as a solace, and he can go about amongst his friends, for which Mistress Purcell has not strength.'

Daniel Purcell was, with his brother Edward, like, yet unlike, my dear master.

There is a difference in musicians; there are those who can execute well on any instrument, but who never make those instruments speak.

They do not give them a voice; for those who bring out their sound have not the power to do so, for they have no message to deliver. I have heard many perform on the organ and harpsichord since the days when I was often kept spellbound by Mr Purcell, but never has anyone thrilled me as he did. Never has anyone awoke in me a like feeling of rapture, of uplifting from the petty cares, ay, and sorrows, of the heart which I have been called upon to endure.

Adelicia Crespion did not frequent the house now that we were sad. She hated anything like gloom and sorrow, and at this time she was full of her admirers and suitors, and had room for little else. Nor did Edmund Pelham often seek me out.

Our relations to each other were less and less like those of lovers. Yet we came to no explanation; and, indeed, what was there to explain?

We were bound by no promises, and thus there was no promise to break. Yet how my heart clung to him. How I longed to speak the word which would bring a decided answer, and yet, on the rare occasions when he was with me, I was dumb. I think I feared to change waning affection into absolute indifference.

We heard of his success at the Temple; that he was looked on as a man who would rise. The Chief Justice had taken notice of him, and had patronised him; and to win favour with Chief Justice Jeffreys was—so it was thought—something to be proud of.

But the terrible stories of his cruel judgments on those who aided and abetted the Duke of Monmouth's rebellion made my heart turn with loathing from this man. He seemed a monster to me. And when, in the September of the previous year, he had been made Lord Chancellor, I was distressed at such promotion. Edmund Pelham, who brought the news in to Mrs Purcell, laughed at me for saying,—

'I would rather weep than rejoice that the Chief Justice is made Lord Chancellor.'

'What! would you have had Monmouth on the throne—the bastard son of the late King. He has met a deserved fate, and so have all those who took up arms for him.'

'What! helpless women—such as Mistress Alice Lisle,' Mr Purcell said. 'Nay, Edmund, I do not agree in that. Jeffreys may be an able and acute lawyer, but he is cruel, and thirsts for blood.'

The fate of the gay and handsome Duke of Monmouth had filled many hearts with pain, yet there was, from all accounts, a want of manliness in him, for he grovelled at King James's feet, and sued in abject terror for pardon and for life.

How widely different from the noble bearing of my Lord Russell when he was unrighteously condemned to die.

It was one of my most ardent desires to see Rachel, Lady Russell. I had invested her with every perfection of form and features. I looked on her as the very personification of loyal wifehood. I caught a glimpse of her this year on her way from Court, where she had gone to plead for restitution of her children's rights, which had been forfeited in consequence of their father's suffering the death of a traitor. A traitor! the very name fills me with indignation when applied to this brave, good man. As I said, I caught a glimpse of Lady Rachel's face, and what beauty she might have had was gone.

Her eyes were bleared and dim with weeping, and her face worn and haggard. The heavy mourning had cast a dark shadow on it, and I keep in my memory a picture of a sad, broken-hearted woman, for whom life had lost its sweetness, and whose happy days were ended for ever.

In this year, 1686, I was for the first time a guest at a wedding. Nothing could persuade Mrs Purcell to attend it. She therefore insisted on my taking her place.

Mr Purcell was not pleased to have me in exchange for his wife as his companion at the wedding of Mr William Mountfort and Mistress Susanna Perceval. He had written a nuptial song for the occasion, and after the ceremony in the church we all repaired to the bride's house, and the guests at the wedding - feast were entertained with music, Mr Purcell's song being sung by the bridegroom, whose clear, musical voice rang out with great power and beauty. I could but notice, young as I was, that there was more sadness than joy in the bridegroom's demeanour, that Mrs Bracegirdle seemed to affect a gladness she did not feel, and that she was pestered by the gross flattery and unwelcome attentions of Captain Hill. He had a boy with him, scarcely more than a child, richly dressed in purple velvet, and ruffles of costly lace. I asked a gentleman who sat next me at the board who the boy might be.

'He is Lord Mohun, and how it is that his guardians can permit him to be led about by that man Captain Hill baffles many who witness it. He will work the boy's ruin. See now how he is drinking more wine than he ought, and how Hill is constantly filling up his cup.'

I watched the boy's flushed face, and heard his

half-drunken laugh at what my neighbour said she knew were ribald jests, and I was sorry for him. He was only a child, but he had learned much of evil, which left its mark even then upon his face, as I learned later, and by the machinations of a man old enough to be his father, he was doomed to the paths of wickedness and sin.

This wedding feast is memorable to me, for I saw Edmund Pelham paying court to a fine lady—an actress, whose face was painted, and who had bold, dark eyes which were darting glances on all sides.

'One of Mistress Bracegirdle's rivals on the stage,' my informant said, 'yonder painted woman, who is getting that handsome gentleman into her toils. Is he not the young man to whom the Lord Chancellor is giving his patronage? Have you any knowledge of him?'

'Yes,' I said.

'What is his name?' was next asked.

'Edmund Pelham.'

'Ah!' she said, seeing my discomfiture, for I could not conceal it. 'Ah! I see you know yonder gentleman very well—mayhap too well.'

I stiffened at once, and turning away, I said,—

'Mr Pelham is a connection of my stepmother's.'

'Do not be affronted,' was the rejoinder, 'I lay a wager you have many suitors.'

Something in me made this sort of talk hateful, and at this wedding-feast there was much of it on every side. I longed to get away from it, as there was no chance of my having any more than a smile and a kind greeting from Mrs Bracegirdle.

I tried to catch Mr Purcell's eye, but he was again at the harpsichord, and Mr Mountfort was again beginning to sing. Then the company rose and the tables were pushed aside, so that the guests might get freely about the room. I happened to get near the bride.

She had a very bright, clever face, and she was leaning on the arm of a gentleman who resembled her.

'This is Mistress Betty Lockwood, I think,' the bride said; 'I have heard of you from my dear friend, Mistress Bracegirdle, and from Master Mountfort also. I am glad you have been a guest at my wedding.' Then turning to her companion, she said, addressing me, 'This is my cousin, Leonard Perceval; he does not often find himself in the society of these vain folks who act plays, which he disapproves and condemns. Is it not so, Leonard?'

A pair of grave eyes were fastened on me, as Mr Perceval said,—

'It is true that I would fain see my cousin wedded

to anyone but an actor; but since it is so, there is
no better to be found than Will Mountfort.'

'Thanks, my good cousin, for your praise of one
who needs none from any man—to know him is
enough.'

The smile with which this was greeted was somewhat sad, I thought, and Mr Perceval said,—

'You deserve the man, Susanna, who needs no
praise from the outside, and, as I said, if you
must wed an actor, none can be better than Mountfort.'

At this moment the bride's father came up to her
and said he wanted to present her to some lord
who was present, and whose name I did not catch.

Then it was that Mr Perceval said,—

'Are you without an escort here, Mistress Lockwood? If it be so, may I have the honour of taking
you under my care?'

'I came hither with Master Henry Purcell,' I
answered, 'at Mistress Purcell's request. She is not
able to appear anywhere at present, being oppressed
with low spirits and sorrow, but—' I hesitated. It
seemed a great deal to ask. However, I took courage and went on—'I should be very thankful to
return to Westminster, if you, sir, would help me to
do so. I am not suited to a company like this.'

'Nor am I,' was the reply. 'I came hither at the

earnest request of my cousin, the bride.   But actors
and actresses are foreign to my taste.'

I was about to add,—

'And to mine,' when I thought of Mrs Bracegirdle,
who was still the object of my devoted admiration.
'There are actresses, sir, who are worthy to be
admired, and with whom it is an honour to be
associated.'

'Yes,' he said, with a sigh; 'you are thinking of
Mistress Bracegirdle, and I assent to what you say
as regards her, but there are—look yonder!'

I followed the direction of his eyes to a recess
where the woman I had seen before talking with
Edmund was now fanning herself and ogling him
with her bold eyes.

The wine had made her garrulous, and she was
talking and laughing loudly, while, to my surprise,
Edmund appeared to relish her jests, and laughed
also, toying with the riband that was tied to a long
tress of hair which lay across the low-cut bodice of
her gown.

'If he can care for such a woman as yonder
painted lady,' I thought, 'it is impossible he can
care for me,' and from that moment I determined
to let Edmund know that I held him by no promise, and he was free.

Something, it may be, in the look I cast towards Edmund and his companion struck Mr Perceval.

'Come away,' he said; 'if you will permit me to do so, I will conduct you to Westminster. Where is Master Purcell's house situated?'

'In Dean's Yard, close to the Abbey.'

I drew the hood of my cloak well over my face and was leaving the now crowded room when Edmund came towards me.

'Whither away, Betty? There will be dancing soon. Do not miss the best part of the revel. I believe you are a veritable Puritan. If so, you should not wear a cherry-coloured lining to your hood,' touching my cheek as he spoke with his finger, adding, 'It is vastly becoming, and gives your face the crimson tinge it needs.'

'It is a better tinge than paint gives,' I said, with emphasis.

'Pshaw! do not be a little prude, Bet; it does not suit you.'

All this time Mr Perceval had stood by, much wondering, I am sure, who it could be who thus made free with his remarks. I was greatly disturbed and the hot colour rushed to my face. But I summoned courage to say,—

'Let Master Purcell know I am tired, and that Mistress Purcell will need me, so I am returning to Dean's Yard under the escort of this gentleman, who is the bride's cousin.'

As I said this it came upon me like a thunder-bolt that it was strange for me, a young maiden, to accept the safe conduct of a gentleman who was a stranger to me.

With ready insight Mr Perceval seemed to read my thoughts, for he said, turning to Edmund,—

'With your permission, sir, I will conduct this young gentlewoman to Master Purcell's house, unless you are disposed to do so.'

I do not know what Edmund might have said had not there been a great stir amongst the guests, and two lacqueys, standing at the door, shouted in loud tones,—

'The Lord Chancellor!'

And in came one of whom I had a picture in my mind which was different from the reality.

The Lord Chancellor was in an amiable mood, and he bowed and smiled to the guests who came fluttering round him, anxious for notice.

William Mountfort was well pleased that he should honour his wedding with his presence, for there was what seemed to many a very extra-ordinary friendship between men of such opposite characters.

He led up his bride to the Lord Chancellor, who

kissed her on the cheek as she made a low curtsey to him, and threw over her neck a glittering gold chain, with jewels that flashed in the sunshine.

Strange it is how the past, be it ever so faultful and deserving of reprobation, of a man called to some high office is forgotten.

As we made our way outside the house, where there was a throng of lacqueys and a crowd staring at the Lord Chancellor's grand gilt coach, Mr Perceval said,—

'It would seem that the horrors of the Bloody Assize are forgotten.'

He spoke in a voice which was audible to others beside me, and a woman who heard what he said sprang forward.

'Forgotten, do you say! the Bloody Assize forgotten! It is written on my heart; it can never die from my memory, for yonder wicked man sent two of my young sons to the scaffold at Lyme, and I have walked over miles of country that I may curse him, yes, curse him! And if I had the strength, I would plunge a sword into his body.'

The poor woman's haggard face was distraught with passion and vengeance.

'She is mad, poor soul!' a man standing near us in the throng said. 'She hurled her curse at my lord as he passed in; he took no heed of it.'

'Not he,' said another; 'he is used to 'em—likes 'em better than blessings, maybe.'

Mr Perceval drew me through the crowd to an empty space, and then I said,—

'Can nought be done for that poor woman? Her terrible face will haunt me!'

'She is one of many like sufferers,' Mr Perceval said. 'I am glad to get away from the sight of that arrogant man, and William Mountfort's attachment to him is a marvel, for Mountfort is tender-hearted, and a man who is full of kindness to all about him. But this union of opposite natures is not infrequent, of which fact, madam, you are too young to have had much experience.'

I was glad when I reached Dean's Yard, and hoped to get into Mr Purcell's house without meeting anyone. I was not so fortunate, for Adelicia Crespion was coming across from the Chanter's house, and waved her hand to me. How provoked and indignant I felt when she said, as she passed me, in a voice which was quite audible,—

'Ah! a new suitor. Where is the old one?'

If Mr Perceval heard, he took no heed of what Adelicia said. He bowed low, and, with his hat in his hand, addressing me, said,—

'I will wish you good day, madam; having seen

you safely to your home, my services are no longer needed.'

If I had not been seized with my accustomed dumbness or diffidence, I should have thanked Mr Perceval for his kindness, and I should have begged him to come in and see Mrs Purcell; but I did neither, and stood, like the confused idiot I was, watching the tall figure disappear under the gateway of Dean's Yard.

Adelicia's laugh was but natural.

'Well-a-day!' she said, 'it was like a scene in a play to see you standing tongue-tied as my fine gentleman made his bow. Who is he? He has no beauty to boast of, and his coat was not cut after the fashion, and his cloak is too long. Have you lost your tongue, child?'

'I am angry with myself, and with you for laughing at me; but I must really go in now,' I said, lifting the latch of the door.

'I am coming in also. I have a lot to say to you, Betty.'

The woman who had of late come to help in the household since Mrs Purcell's illness now came into the passage.

'The mistress is asleep,' she said. 'She has had a visit from the old dame, the master's mother and that always brings about a fit of

G

megrims. She is quiet now; don't go and wake her.'

I went into the parlour, followed by Adelicia, who flung herself on the settle, saying,—

'I am sick of the world; sick of everything; sick of myself.'

'You do not look as if this were true,' I said. 'You look well enough, and content, too.'

Instead of answering me, Adelicia said,—

'How is it with you and Edmund Pelham?'

This was a hard question.

'We are friends,' I said.

'Friends! Pshaw! You are lovers. Don't be a fool, Betty; tell me the truth.'

Thus pressed, I said,—

'What is your reason for wishing to pry into my affairs?'

'That's a queer thing to ask me, when we have been friends all this time.'

'I have not seen much proof of your friendship of late,' I said. 'You have scarcely acted like a friend.'

'Do you know why?' and to my surprise—my great surprise—Adelicia burst into tears. 'Do you know why? It is because, if I had sought you out often, I should have had worse fits of remorse than I have, which need not be. A worse traitor than I am can't exist.'

I did not really understand what Adelicia meant, but a light began to dawn on me. A traitor! What did she mean?

'Well,' I said, 'tell me how you have been treacherous to me.'

'I have let—I have liked—I have been happy to suffer Edmund Pelham to make desperate love to me. There, it is out now; hate me, despise me as you will; you know the truth.'

Now, however much a woman may assure herself that she sees a love once fervent for her waning, and assure herself also that she is ready to accept with a good grace what is inevitable, it is ever a bitter lesson for her to learn. And it was still more bitter in my case, when the main cause of Edmund's declining love for me was the fact that all these months he had acted a double part. Why had he not been honest and told me that he had seen in Adelicia one more suited to him than I was? After all, we were bound by no promise, and he need not have put me off as he had often done, and persisted that I was his dear little Betty, whom he loved still.

Adelicia rocked herself to and fro, and, as I did not speak, she sobbed out,—

'I've not told you all. My uncle wants me to marry an old prebendary, Master Berkeley. He thinks this an honour for me, and the Dean approves, and gave me his blessing t'other night. The notion of it! I want none of his blessing, though he is a Bishop and Dean in one. But, Betty—dear, sweet Betty—I am in such a strait; help me out of it.'

'How can I help you?' I said coldly.

'By telling Edmund.'

'What am I to tell him?'

'That I don't want to marry old Berkeley.'

'And you do want to marry him.' I felt at this time nothing but contempt for Adelicia—so mean, so pitiful did her conduct seem. But I controlled myself, and only said, 'I will do your bidding. And now I must go to Mistress Purcell, for I have been about all day, and she will want me.'

'And you will not kiss me, nor forgive me, Betty?'

'We will not speak of forgiveness,' I said, 'nor, indeed, of anything more now.'

'You are cruel,' Adelicia sobbed. 'I did not think you would be so cruel.'

I left the parlour, and Adelicia to her own reflections, which could not have been very agreeable ones, methinks.

Mrs Purcell wanted to hear of the wedding, and whether Mr Purcell's song received the praise it deserved.

'I do not like these actors and actresses,' Mrs
Purcell said, 'and I would that Henry had less to
do with them. They keep him out late at night,
and he is always at their beck and call to compose for them. William Mountfort is the best of
them.'

'And Mistress Bracegirdle,' I said. 'You should
have seen her to-day. It is not that she is so
beautiful that few can compare with her, but she
has the purest face, and eyes that are as clear
as the heavens above.'

'You always talk of Mistress Bracegirdle as if
she were an angel, child. If she is, she has caused
much mischief by her angelic beauty, and will
cause more ere she has done.'

'I think she has done good—more good than
harm — but then I know nothing of the world,
actors or others.'

'She makes wives unhappy when they see their
husbands enthralled by her beauty and acting, as
many are.'

I wondered if she meant to refer to my dear
master. Surely not, for we soon heard his step
on the stairs, and he came in with his arms
outstretched, saying,—·

'How is my sweet heart?—better, I trust. I
missed you sorely at the wedding feast; and this

little Betty ran off with a gentleman, the bride's cousin, though she calls him brother.'

'An actor also, no doubt.'

'Nay, a deacon in the Church; so you are wrong, Frances. I hear he is soon to be fully ordained, and will have a cure in Hertfordshire, which has been promised him by the patron. No, no, Betty did not run off with an actor this time, though we cannot tell what she may do some fine day. Eh, Betty?'

'I think actors may be as good as any other men,' I said. 'Master Mountfort surely is good.'

'Ay, that he is, but he has, like most of us, two sides to him. The side which makes him the sworn friend of Jeffreys is one I do not understand. But the friendship betwixt them seems thicker than ever. To-day the Lord Chancellor strutted about with his hand in Mountfort's arm, filling some of the sycophants who were hanging about with envy. Now I must away to make progress with my ode to King James, and call the tuneful Muses to my aid. Verily is it true the King never dies, and so we poor musicians know, for, Charles or James, it is all the same—we must commemorate the reigning monarch as soon as we have buried the dead out of our sight. They tell me my wild "Lillibullero" is much liked. I heard an urchin in the street shouting the tune and stamping his clogs to the time.'

'Lillibullero' Mr Purcell hummed as he ran downstairs.

He was so young and joyous in those years, full of spirit, not yet quenched by weakness of body, which came to him all too soon, and which gave to his later compositions a vein of sadness the earlier themes did not know.

I did not see Edmund Pelham for some days, and I heard no more of Adelicia. But, as I was hastening across Dean's Yard from evensong one day, I heard steps behind me, evidently of someone who would fain overtake me. In another moment the Chanter, Mr Crespion, was at my side.

'Mistress Lockwood, I desire a few words of conversation with you. Be so obliging as to step into my house.'

It may seem strange, but it is true, that the Abbey dignitaries held themselves very much apart and above those not connected with the august body of Dean and Chapter. It will be said that my dear master, holding the position of organist, was really a member of that body. It is true; but, indebted as the Chapter (as it was called) was to the genius of their organist, they made him understand there was a gulf fixed between them and him. He was their paid servant, and had to do their bidding.

'Step in, Mistress Lockwood,' the Chanter said, taking off his shovel hat and giving his surplice into the care of his servant, for the Chanter and prebendaries always robed in their own houses, and walked to the Abbey in their surplices over their cassocks. 'Step in.' And then, opening the door of a dark parlour, Mr Crespion said, 'Be seated. I think you are well acquainted with my niece, Mistress Adelicia Crespion?'

'Yes, sir ; that is the case.'

'She is giving me much trouble and anxiety. She has a suitor of whom I approve, and I am proud to say his Lordship of Rochester, who is also the valued Dean of this Abbey of Westminster, gives his sanction to the union. But I grieve to say my niece is contumacious, and vows she will not wed with Master Berkeley. It is madness, sheer madness. She has not a penny piece in the world, and yet refuses, nay, scoffs in an unseemly manner, at the good and worthy gentleman who does her the honour to seek her for his wife. Now I ask you, Mistress Lockwood, to do your utmost to convince this little vixen of her folly, and assure her, if she persists in disobeying my commands, I cannot permit her to remain under my roof. I ask you, therefore, to do my bidding to the best of your power, and persuade Adelicia to yield consent to my wishes.'

As usual, my words were slow in coming, and I was sorely puzzled to know what I should say to the reverend gentleman, who stood with his cassock turned over one arm, and with the other patting his bag-wig, which had got a bit awry when he removed his hat.

'I have,' he went on, 'a true regard for Master Henry Purcell, and I take it you are of kin to him, and that I may trust you to endeavour to break this foolish young woman's obstinate will.'

'I am not of kin, sir,' I replied, 'to Master Henry Purcell. I came to his house by the intervention of Master Gostling.'

'Ah, a good friend of mine, with a voice such as has rarely sounded in the Chapel Royal. But proceed.'

'I came, sir, from a home which was scarce a home by reason of a harsh stepmother, to be of service to Mistress Purcell, who has indifferent health.'

'Yes, yes, poor woman. Those infants of hers are only born to die. So you are—a—a—well, what in a large household of the nobility we call a lady-in-waiting.'

'I have no such post, sir; I assist in all domestic matters which fall to me, and it is my highest

pleasure to do what I can for those who are very
good to me.   Moreover, there is the music ; it is a
rich reward to live in a home where the air is full
of music—and such music ! '

The Chanter smiled benignly on me.

' Ah !' he said, 'and what instrument do you play ? '

' I have learned the harpsichord, sir, by my
master's goodness in now and again giving me
instruction; but I have but little time to spare,
and what time I have I give to making copies of
Master Purcell's score.'

We had wandered away from the subject which
was uppermost in our minds, and the Chanter said,
somewhat pompously,—

' My niece must make a marriage fitted to '—he
hesitated a little, and gave a short cough—'fitted, I
say, to *my* position, which, you are aware, is an
important one, as Chanter of the Abbey of Westminster.   I fear my niece has taken some foolish
fancy into her head, and I shall be obliged to you
to discover what it is, and report it to me.'

' I venture to say, sir, that, with all due respect to
you, I should not covet the office of finding out
Mistress Crespion's intentions, in order to report
them to you.'

' Indeed !' the Chanter said, with added dignity.
' Indeed !   Then this interview is fruitless, and I

must wish you good-evening. Make my compliments to Mistress Purcell, and say I wish her better health.'

I retraced my steps across Dean's Yard with some uneasiness. Had I acted aright—and was it wrong on my part to leave the Chanter in ignorance of what I knew—that Adelicia was in love with Edmund Pelham?

I had half determined to go back and say I had a notion of the obstacle which lay in the way of Adelicia's acceptance of Mr Berkeley's suit, when the person most interested in the matter came gaily towards me.

'How fares it with you, Betty?' Edmund said. 'I swear I never saw you look better than at the wedding—William Mountfort's wedding. I came with a request—that you will allow me to conduct you to the theatre on the morrow, to see the fair Bracegirdle as Ophelia in "Hamlet." You used to recite poor, distraught Ophelia's speech in the days when I first read the play to you— Well, what is wrong?'

'I have something that I must say to you, Edmund. Dearly as I should love to see Mistress Bracegirdle as Ophelia, I cannot come to the theatre with you.'

'Now, I vow you shall come. Do not turn Puritan, Betty, and scout immortal Shakespeare as an agent of the Evil One.'

'If you will step into the parlour I will give you some reasons other than those you imagine for my refusal of your request.'

'They must be good ones, or I will not entertain them.'

By good fortune the parlour was empty. There was a choir practice proceeding in the opposite room, and there will never be a moment in my life when the air of, 'Ah! how sweet it is to love,' from the music by Mr Purcell for Dryden's tragedy, 'Tyrannic Love,' will not awake the remembrance of the time when Edmund Pelham stood before me, as I said,—

'I hear from Adelicia Crespion—'

Immediately his face grew pale, but he interrupted me by saying,—

'What! Has she been filling your mind with one of her romances?'

'It is no romance,' I said ; 'it is unvarnished truth. She tells me you have been for months at her feet as her lover.'

'One of many if I have,' he said lightly.

'However that may be, you are the favoured suitor, and she is obstinately refusing to wed a gentleman chosen for her by her uncle—his reverence, the Chanter, Master Crespion.'

'May I venture to inquire where you have gained this intelligence?'

'From her own lips as to your love for her, and from Master Crespion as to her refusal to marry Master Berkeley. There can be no mistake in the matter, Edmund. I only desire to see you free from any tie that may have existed between us. I know you were not bound to me, and yet, without a promise given, I had faith in you, and in the love you professed to entertain for me.'

I began to fear I should break into tears, and this would have been humiliating, so I hastened to come to an end of what I had to say.

It was notable that Edmund was really unable to make any defence. I can pity him as I remember now how he stood toying with the riband of his sword-hilt and with a look of set defiance on his handsome face, turning on me now and again glances from his lustrous eyes, which were more angry than reproachful.

'So be it,' he said at last. 'I befriended you, Betty, when you were friendless. I did my utmost to see your gifts of mind and intellect, which were neglected by your stepmother, cultivated.'

'I know it,' I said. 'I was not ungrateful, and Edmund, I loved you—'

'Then nothing shall, I swear, come between us he said, making an effort to seize my hand.

'Something *has* come between us,' I said. 'Do you imagine that I will be treacherous to Adelicia? You must be mad if you think I can hold to you while I know you have been stealing the heart of another woman. Only I thank God I have found out in time that truth and honour are to you but empty names.'

'Upon my life, Betty, I did not expect you to be such a queen of tragedy; you will rival the fair Bracegirdle. You had better take to the stage. Well, I take my dismissal, and must needs do it with a good grace.'

He made as if he were leaving the room, and through the half open door came the sound of

'Ah! how sweet it is to love,'

sung by the pure, sweet treble of one of the choristers of the Chapel Royal.

'Ah! how sweet it is to love.' The words left my lips before I was aware, and I added, 'Ah! how bitter to be deceived.'

'Wait one moment, Edmund,' I said, 'to hear one last word. Go to Master Crespion and declare your love for Adelicia. Be honest and true to her and to yourself, and may God speed your suit and bless you.'

I think there never was a revolution of feeling such as I then witnessed and experienced. Edmund shut the door, and flung himself on his knees before me.

'You are an angel, Betty, and I am a traitor. I thought you but a child, and I find you are a woman—a noble woman. Forgive me, Betty, forgive me, and pray for one who is easily tempted. Do not be hard in your judgment, Betty, I will do your bidding. I will make a clean breast of it to the Chanter. If he kicks me out of his house, I shall only meet my deserts, for Adelicia is already my wife. I married her secretly yester morning.'

This was indeed a final blow, and I could only clasp my hands in an agony of entreaty.

'Do not delay,' I said. 'Oh! I beseech you, do not delay, and go straight to the Chanter's house. I pray you leave me, Edmund, I have no more strength left in me.'

'I will do your bidding,' he said, 'and may God forgive me for the wrong I have wrought on the innocent.'

So he left me. I do not know how long I lay unconscious on the settle.

I knew no more till I felt Mrs Purcell's gentle hand on my forehead, and the woman who tended her loosing my girdle. It was the first time Mrs

Purcell had come into the parlour from her chamber
above, and I was distressed to see how pallid and
ill she looked.

'What is it, Betty?' she asked. 'You were
on the floor, when we found you, in a deep
swoon.'

'I cannot tell you now,' I said, 'not now,' and
the blessed relief of tears was granted me.

Those of my descendants who have perchance
seen the fall of their idols, who have known the
pain of being deceived, who have, in the days of
early youth, given their love to one who had first
stirred an answering love in their hearts, will know
what was the pain I endured. But let them take
courage.

This is a sorrow which passes like all earthly
troubles of whatever kind. Such is the blessed
order of Him who rules our lives. We must
needs confess that time heals the wound, and as
we look back on the past we often have cause
to be thankful that there is a 'divinity which
shapes our ends, rough hew them how we will.'
I have come to be thankful for what seemed at
first a grief which could know no balm, for betrayal is ever bitter, and is a sword which
pierces with a deeper wound than change or loss
of those we love by death.

I have known both sorrows, and I bear my testimony to the bitterness of the first, and the consolations which spring from the last. Just as from a dry root, apparently dead to all outward things, but wakened to life once more by the blessed dew from heaven and the rays of sunshine, so from dead hopes will often spring comfort and blessings which in hours of darkness and distress we little dreamed could ever be ours again.

H

BOOK III

1687—1688

'Guide your life towards a single course of action, and if every action goes its due length, as far as may be, rest contented.'—MARCUS AURELIUS.

CHAPTER V

A. D. 1687

THIS year passed without any great change to mark it in my life.

The Chanter having come once to storm in a manner wholly undignified as to his niece's marriage, accusing me of complicity therewith, and even venting his wrath upon Mr Purcell, we heard no more of him on that score.

For some time he was disposed to be mightily uncivil to Mr Purcell, thwarting him with regard to the music in the Abbey services, and condemning anthems and chants from, as it seemed, sheer perversity. For the Chanter in a cathedral body has great power, as it falls to him to settle the music for the organist and choir. In most cases the Chanter's office is a mere sinecure, but it was not so in the Abbey of Westminster. Mr Crespion professed to be a judge of music, and to be in a position to find fault with the selections which were submitted to him for approval. My dear master would sometimes come from his interviews with the Chanter in great heat and vexation; but his sweet temper generally gained the victory, and he would soon forget his irritation and resort to his music, forgetting, maybe, that his devotion to it was often the cause of the Chanter's displeasure. Sometimes my master would laugh to himself as he sat putting into shape some new composition, pushing towards me a sheet of score to copy full of alterations since the first was made.

He said one day,—

'His reverence the Chanter will scoff at this "pastoral elegy," Betty, as he scoffs at most of my compositions, but herein lies the difference between him and me—he but *hears* the music while I *feel* it. Why, did I lose my hearing to-morrow, which God forbid! I could still compose; I could still feel what I craved to make others feel. I should yet have the secret joy which thousands of people, who pretend to adore music, know nothing of. Music is a coy mistress, Betty, and gives herself to those whom she holds with silken fetters. Methinks you are one of them, Betty!'

I could not but be surprised to hear my master

say this—I, who could play but indifferently well
on the harpsichord.

'Hearken, Betty; too often it is not those who
can run over with deft fingers the keyboard of an
organ who know best what music means. Forsooth, when Master Gostling fancies he is making
music on the viol di gamba, I can scarce hinder
myself from snatching it from him and bidding
him use only the instrument God has given him
—his splendid bass voice—in the place of zinging
and zilting and twanging on that vile viol di
gamba.'

I knew in part what my dear master said then.
I know it well now, for age has not deprived me
of the power of melting into tenderness or rising
to joyousness, or of being touched to tears by the
pathos, as the case may be, of which some music
discourses, apart from any words to which it may
be wedded.

It was well for me in the year following the
treachery of my lover and my so-called friend that
I had so much to divert my thoughts from self-
pity in Mr Purcell's house. Many came and went,
and amongst them, a frequent guest, was Mr
William Mountfort and his wife, at whose wedding
feast I met her cousin, Mr Perceval.

I said, and truly, that this year 1687 was uneventful as far as my own life was concerned, yet I must not forget that I saw in the autumn Mrs Bracegirdle as Ophelia, and so enthralled was I with the personation of that maiden with her unrequited love that I verily saw her before me, and never once thought of Mrs Bracegirdle. The lovely, distraught creature before me, with the tangle of wildflowers in her hair, some hanging loosely amidst her beautiful tresses, was Ophelia.

Her song—the song of a broken heart—is in my ears now, not as I have heard it since many a time and oft, but as it rang out in the clear, sweet, mournful tones of her who was then Ophelia —living, breathing Ophelia,—

> ' They bore him barefaced on the bier,
> And on his grave rains many a tear.'

Then how she stayed her song for a few moments and said,—

'There's rosemary; that's for remembrance, pray, love, remember; and there's pansies, that's for thoughts. There's fennel for you, and columbines ; and there's rue for you, and here's some for me.'

Sure, in the voice that pronounced these words, 'There's rue for you and *some for me*,' was there the foreshadowing of the day when there was rue indeed for her who now personated Ophelia.

Tears rained down my face as she broke forth
again into a weird chant of despairing grief,—

'And will he not come again?
And will he not come again?
No, no; he is dead.
Go to thy death-bed,
He never will come again.'

When they brought in, with procession of priests
and king and queen, the fair corpse of Ophelia,
lying on her bier with all her tangled tresses and
wildflowers over her for a pall, I cried out,—

'Oh! it is too pitiful!   Why did no one save her?'

'Silence!' was the harsh reprimand from a man
who sat near me. 'Silence!'

I was silent then.   But so real was the scene to
me that I sat with clasped hands and bowed head,
wondering how, between the acts, the people could
laugh and jest and chatter of a thousand idle
matters.

At the conclusion of the play, Mrs Purcell and I
were bidden to sup with Mr Mountfort and his wife.

There we found Mrs Bracegirdle, and as I entered
she held out her hands to me, saying,—

'Ah! Come hither, child; your words, which
reached my ears as I lay upon the bier, were sweeter
to me than a thousand plaudits. See,' she said, 'I
will give you this bit of rosemary for remembrance,

but there shall be no rue for you, dear child. That
is for me;' and separating the rue from the rest of
the flowers, she put it in her bosom with a sigh.

The sad mood soon passed, and she was bright
and gay, exchanging jests with Mr William Mountfort, and looking so beautiful and fair I could not
marvel at the adoring glances cast upon her.

All wanted to win a word or smile from her,
and I drew into the background; and it was Mrs
Susanna Mountfort who made room for me next
her on the bench at the supper board.

'You think yonder lady lovely,' she said, looking
in the direction of the head of the board, where
Mrs Bracegirdle sat, with Mr Mountfort on her
right side.

'Yes,' I said. 'Never did I see anyone so beautiful.'

'Few have seen any in her place so good and
pure. I know her better than most folks, and I
could tell you deeds of charity of which hundreds
who look at her on the stage know nought. I
have seen her go forth on her errand of mercy in
Clare Market to succour the poor and needy, to
distribute alms to the old and feeble ones who can
no longer earn their livelihood. At times my father
has accompanied her, fearing she might have insults
or even rough handling in the crowd of the destitute,
but he finds she needs no protection. As she passes

along, the thankful acclamations of the people of all degrees greet her ears. If anyone dared to affront her, my father says he would be torn to pieces at once. Ah!' Mrs Mountfort said, 'affronts and insults do not come to Mistress Bracegirdle from the poor and the needy; they are offered by those who are of higher rank. My husband strives to be her shield and protector from the wicked machinations of evil men. Maybe you will hear people say that Will's devotion to Mistress Bracegirdle is other than that of the purest friendship. You may give them the lie. My Will is true as steel, and his heart's love is given to me, a wife who is all unworthy of it. Great changes are at hand for us. Will thinks of abandoning the stage for a while to live with the Lord Chancellor, who, in his gilded state, craves for the company of one who is faithful to him. It amazes me at times to think Will can be the friend of the Chancellor. Many shudder at the very sound of his name, and talk of the Bloody Assize as a red stain on him, which nothing he may do later can wash away. But my Will has the gift of ever finding out the best in everyone, and being blind to the worst. See!' Mrs Mountfort broke off, 'who comes here?'

I looked towards the door, and saw, to my distress, that Edmund and Adelicia were being introduced by that evil-looking man whose name was Hill. I hoped neither Edmund nor his wife would discover me. They received but a cold welcome from Mrs Bracegirdle, who said, in her clear, ringing voice, now touched with disdain,—

'To what am I indebted for the honour of this visit, Captain Hill? I fear me you come in for but the end of a feast.'

'Which, fairest lady, is better than the beginning of a fray,' was Captain Hill's rejoinder. 'I venture to introduce my friends, Master Edmund Pelham of the Inner Temple, and his lady.'

Mrs Bracegirdle bowed.

'Find places for this gentleman and his lady at the further end of the board, Master Mountfort, and see that they are served with such viands as may be left.'

Thus it was that Edmund and Adelicia found themselves near me and Mrs Mountfort.

I had not spoken to either of them since they had so shamefully deceived me, but I showed less confusion than they did, I think.

Edmund rallied more quickly than Adelicia. She looked so thin and ill, I could but be sorry for her. Her cheeks were painted, and her whole appearance that of a woman of fashion.

She was dressed fantastically, even in excess

of the *mode*, and she flirted her fan and played with her ribands to hide what was evident confusion.

Edmund addressed himself to Mrs Mountfort, praised her husband's acting, spoke of his friendship for the Chancellor, and said he had been so good as to further his interests by speaking to him of his desire to succeed at the Bar.

Adelicia rattled on in a confused manner, and I was at a loss to understand what she meant. She did not refer at first to the past, and it was not for me to do so.

But just as Mrs Purcell came up to tell me the time had come to take our leave, Adelicia said, in a low voice,—

'I wish you did not hate me, Betty. Say one good word to me. Say you forgive me.'

'Yes,' I answered, 'I can say as much from my heart; but there is an end—'

'No, no, not an end. See me sometimes. I— I am not well. I have a bad cough, and I think I am going to die.'

Edmund had watched us from across the board, and now, rising, said hastily,—

'Get into your hood and cloak, Adelicia; we must take our departure.'

At the door, where there was some confusion

the guests calling for their chairs, and the link-boys hustling each other to be the first to be hired, I was next Edmund.

'I am glad to see you looking well,' he said. 'I was at Ivy Farm this day sennight. Mistress Lockwood is stricken with some sore disease. You will soon be in possession there.'

'I do not understand you,' I said.

'Is that possible? In the due order of things, at Mistress Lockwood's death, Ivy Farm will be yours.'

'It is not a near prospect, I hope,' I said. 'Good-night, Edmund!'

'You will never forgive me, I see,' he said. 'Nor do I think I merit forgiveness. As for Adelicia, poor soul! she is wearing herself to a skeleton, whether from remorse or disappointment I cannot say.' He took my hand for an instant in his own, and was about to kiss it, but I drew it away. 'Unforgiving,' he murmured. 'Well, so be it.'

I remember, as if it were but yesterday, how sweet it was to me to return after the exciting play of 'Hamlet,' and the supper that followed it, to Dean's Yard.

Westminster has a peculiar charm for me; and now, in my old age, I repair thither at times to think over my past life, so small and insignificant as it appears when compared with the great past

of kings and queens, statesmen and patriots, which
in the records of the Abbey lay before me as in
an open book.

And it fell to my share to see laid to rest
within these sacred walls those with whom the
days of my youth were spent, and whom I held
in undying love and reverence.

Mrs Purcell had seen me speaking to Edmund
Pelham, and said,—

'I marvel that you should hold any conversation
with that man, Betty. Sure he has proved himself
to be unworthy of all respect. That poor thing,
his wife, has a sorry time of it, I expect. I heard
t'other day that Master Pelham lives more in his
Temple chambers than with her, who, on pretence
of her health, he has put up in a cottage at Putney.
You have had a great deliverance, Betty.'

If I had, I did not care to hear it; and I began
to praise Mrs Bracegirdle, saying,—

'I could scarce bear to see her act often, it was
so real to me.'

'Ah!' Mrs Purcell said, with a sigh, 'I would
that Henry felt the like. The company of these
actors and actresses is not wholesome. They often
keep him late at taverns and coffee-houses, where
one and another begs him to set some song or
rhyme to music.' And then, with that touch of

pride in her husband which was always there, though often hidden, she said, 'And what wonder! for who is there to compare with him as a musician? I think he is without a rival, and so do you, Betty.'

'Yes,' I answered. 'There is no other hand that wakes in me what I cannot put into words.'

'No,' Mrs Purcell said thoughtfully. 'No, Betty, there are no words which express it. Do not try to do so.'

CHAPTER VI

A.D. 1688

IT was a January day in this year that Mr Purcell came in to tell Mrs Purcell that he had the King's orders to compose an anthem, to be performed on the twenty-fifth day of this month—a thanksgiving day for the prospect of an heir to the Crown, which prospect had been for some time deemed unlikely.

'I must do His Majesty's bidding,' my dear master said, 'though, methinks, it is a somewhat strange command.'

Mrs Purcell smiled and said,—

'You can think of me, dear heart, as you write the music.'

'Ah! that will I,' was the reply, 'and the thought of our promised joy shall quicken my muse and add to the music a double joyance.'

'Be not too sure of that,' was the answer, 'so often has our sadness been the quick follower of joy.'

I

'Nay, I will not have you hopeless, sweet heart, I feel assured God will grant us the blessing we desire; and so past sorrows will be thrown aside, to be remembered no more.'

'As if I could ever forget our dear infant boys, who were born but to die,' Mrs Purcell said, when the master left the parlour. 'A mother's heart can never cease to mourn for her lost children, as you will know some day, Betty.'

It was about this time that Mrs Mountfort came with her cousin, Mr Perceval, who was now an ordained clergyman, and had a cure, as it turned out, not far from my old home of Ivy Farm.

Indeed, this was the cause of his coming to see me.

'I have lately,' he said, 'Mistress Lockwood, been called to minister to a gentlewoman whose house lies within the bounds of the parish next to that of Barton. She is the widow of your father, and she bids me bring you a message to the effect that she suffers great pain, and would fain see you ere she departs this life. The house and farm, as I understand, belong to you. These children of Mistress Lockwood's former marriage have no right to them. I gather this from her own words.'

I was so greatly surprised to hear this from Mr Perceval's lips, and so amazed to find he had aught

to do with my stepmother, that I was, as usual
with me under strong emotion, unable to frame
any words.

Mr Perceval saw my distress, which I doubt not
my face betrayed, and said,—

'As far as I can trust the physician who has been
called to certify the opinion of the village apothecary, there is no danger to life for some time.   Her
great suffering may be prolonged for many weeks
or months.'

'Is my stepmother tended by anyone with care
and kindness?' I asked.

'Yes, the old servant does her best, but she is
untaught, and, it strikes me, somewhat rough with
her mistress.'

'Where are the children?'

'The elder ones are provided for, and, by the intervention of Mr Gostling, sent to the docks as
recruits for the navy, which, it seems, may soon be
called into action.   There is one girl—a wild, harum-
scarum child—but the boy who was next her in age
is dead.'

'Tommy—so full of pranks and naughty ways
—dead!' I exclaimed.

'His mother seems to have made an idol of
him, and it is since his death that she says she
has softened to all the world, and chiefly to you.'

'Would she desire me to go and tend her now she is sick?' I asked.

'I think she would,' was the reply.

I was in a great strait. I felt I could not leave Mrs Purcell now she would need me more than ever, and I shrank from going to Ivy Farm to put up with what I should have to suffer there, for my poor stepmother had ever a violent temper and dislike to me.

'Think well over what you will do,' Mr Perceval said; 'and if I may venture to say so, let me ask you to pray for guidance.'

Now Mrs Mountfort, who had been talking to Mrs Perceval, said,—

'What solemn talk are you having in that corner? My good cousin Leonard is always too grave and sober for his years. To see him in that cassock and bands and shovel hat, he might have come out of the ark. He thinks us poor actors beneath him, and will scarce give Will a smile when he cracks his best jokes.'

'These are not days to laugh and be merry, Sue, or to weep at fictitious sorrows and troubles. There is an undercurrent of dissatisfaction with the popish doings of the King, which is like a smouldering fire that will burst into a flame ere long.'

'It is ill done to meet trouble half way; for my

part, I think we are very well off with our handsome,
gracious King, and a Queen like Mary of Modena.
Sure, they may worship God in their own fashion.'

'I will not argue with you, Susanna, for I greatly
fear indifference is the secret of your tolerance.
Broken promises as to the maintenance of the Protestant faith are not likely to establish confidence
in King James.'

'You are a wiseacre, I know full well, Leonard,
and far above a poor mortal like me. You think me
a wicked actress. You are a thorough-going Puritan
at heart; a pity you did not live when that arch-
traitor Cromwell was in power—you would have
found favour with him. But I do not desire to
quarrel with you. If you have finished your errand
to Mistress Lockwood, we will betake ourselves to
the Haymarket, for I have a rehearsal to attend, and
Will never forgives non-appearance.'

'I will come again ere long,' were Mr Perceval's
parting words, 'and give you further tidings of the
state of things at Ivy Farm.'

I laid the matter before Mrs Purcell as to whether
it was my duty to go to my stepmother, who had
treated me with scant kindness, and had, after a
fashion, robbed me of my rights.

She wept and mourned at the notion of my departure, and I was in a sore strait.

Mrs Purcell talked as if I was a deserter, and about to leave her when she needed me most.

The smallpox was on every hand, she said, and she might fall a victim any day. In her present circumstances she would surely die.

I do not know how things would have been decided had not my dear master taken my part, and at last it was arranged that I should go to Ivy Farm and return before the time Mrs Purcell looked for the birth of her child. How much in all our lives hangs upon the decision we make on what seems a small matter.

I went off one chill February morning to the stage waggon which was to set me down at night at the hostel from which I had started four years before. I had gone forth a child and I was returning a woman. The bitter lesson of betrayal where I had trusted had been given me to learn, and though the wound had healed the scar remained.

The long day's journey was uneventful, and I slept for the greater part of it, being worn out with the pain I felt at leaving Westminster and the sorrow it caused my good friend, Mrs Purcell.

Mr Purcell's mother came to take my place in some measure, and resting on the promise of my return, my dear master was cheerful and encouraged me that I was doing my duty.

Mr Perceval met me with a lanthorn at the hostel, and carried my bundle for me, treating me with great kindness and consideration.

'It was plainly your duty,' he said, 'to come hither, and I am confident you will have a reward.'

'I do not know how that will come about,' I said. 'It is not as though my stepmother had been loving and good to me.'

'Ah!' he said, 'if she had been good and kind you would have missed the reward I speak of.' I did not answer, and Mr Perceval added, 'The reward which is the crown of self-sacrifice. Do you not remember Him who first showed us the way to win that crown?'

I gave but an uncertain assent. My faith in those days was but dim and flickering, and I never could bring myself to profess what I did not really feel.

I had come to my old home with unwilling steps, and the crown my friend spoke of did not shine brightly before me in the future. It was rather a crown of prickly thorns that I wore in the long, long weeks when I watched by the awful suffering which my stepmother was called to endure. I had to hearken to her cries of anguish and her lamentations and sorrow for her injustice to me.

Mr Perceval, whose pleasant rectory house was within a mile or two of Ivy Farm, was frequently with us.

From his lips, nay, rather from his life, I first learned what religion really meant, and Sunday after Sunday I led Madge across the field to the church where he ministered, and drew comfort from what I heard from him.

Madge, with the impetuous ardour of an undisciplined child, conceived the greatest affection for me, and old Rhoda said I was the very first person whom the child had ever obeyed.

Poor, wild, little Madge, with her dark eyes and raven hair, with her russet skin, brown from constant exposure to the air, awoke my pity, and I could not be insensible to her devotion to me.

Nothing could persuade her to be with her poor mother. She would sometimes look into the chamber where she lay, and then rush away again, saying to me,—

'I hate to see sick folks. And when Tommy took ill with a bad throat I ran away and lived with old Goody Hodgkin till he was dead and buried.'

'And if you took ill with a bad throat, would you wish me to run away and leave you?'

'No,' came very decidedly; 'and I know you wouldn't run away.'

'Why do you know it?'

'Because Rhoda says you are an angel, and angels are good; the parson says they watch over us though we cannot see them.' Then she broke into a sudden ripple of laughter. 'I don't believe an angel watches over me. I am too wicked.'

'The more reason you should want one,' I said.

'I've got *you*,' was the answer; 'that is enough.'

As the days lengthened and the spring awoke, my poor stepmother declined. She seemed to have no power to fight against the dire disease which sapped her strength away.

The old arrogant temper was lulled to rest, and she became gentle as a little child.

She clung to me in a manner that touched me beyond words, and now that I look back on those days when I tended her, I am thankful I went to her as duty pointed the way.

And now, I must confess that something sweeter than aught I had ever known before crept into my life.

The constant care and even tenderness with which Mr Perceval surrounded me could not be mistaken. And yet, I dare scarcely trust myself to let him know that I was not indifferent to him.

I could not forget my blind love for Edmund Pelham; how that night in the porch, when he lay at my feet, I believed in the endurance of his promised love for me. I could not forget, and, though I knew I had forgiven him, I likened myself to one who had put to sea in a ship that had been vouched for as seaworthy, but had gone to pieces in the first storm it had encountered; so that when again a voyage was proposed, the venture seemed too great, and hesitation took the place of the assurance with which the first had been undertaken, and the past distress made the future safety appear dim and uncertain.

Yet sure there was an air of truthfulness and honesty in Mr Perceval which was enough to calm all fears and doubts, yet I could not bring myself to accept what he offered me. I could only tell him, with faltering lips, my story, and beg him to be patient with me.

'I will serve seven years for you, if needs be,' he said. 'I am content to wait.'

And I could only thank him with tears, and say that it might be he would find one more suited to him.

I had said the same thing before with no sort of fear that it would come true, and yet how soon what I had in my secret heart thought unlikely, happened.

I had heard and seen but little of Edmund and Adelicia for the past year.

Now and again, as I have related, I saw them when I was in the company of the actors and actresses,

amongst whom Mrs Bracegirdle shone as a bright
star, but all intimate communication had ceased.

It was one fair spring evening, when I was keeping
my accustomed watch by my poor stepmother's bed,
that Madge came rushing in, saying,—

'There's a woman at the door who will see you;
Rhoda can't get her away. She says she is not a
beggar, for she has a fine cloak and hood.'

I bid the child send Rhoda up to take my place
by her mistress, and I would come and find out what
the woman wanted of me.

'She is crying and sobbing as if her heart was
breaking,' Rhoda said, when I met her on the stair;
'but, Lord! it may be sham to get pity. I can
make nought of her, and when I bid her begone, she
rated at me and said she would force me to let
her pass.'

I went to the kitchen door, where Rhoda's husband was keeping guard, with the old sheep dog
at his heels. He made a grimace at me and
whispered,—

'You take care; she is only fit for Bedlam.'

I bid him stand back and then I saw a woman
leaning heavily, as if from exhaustion, against the
half-open door, supporting herself by clutching it
with her hand.

'Come in and rest,' I said, 'and you shall have

a cup of cider, and you shall tell me what has be-
fallen you.'

The woman unfastened her hood, and as it was
loosened I saw a face terribly scarred by the marks
with which we were all too well acquainted—the
cruel marks left by that scourge smallpox, when,
as but seldom it spared life, it printed indelible
and awful traces on the fairest countenances.

'Betty! Betty!' she gasped, 'do you not know
me? No, no, how should you know me as I am?'

The voice—though even that was changed, and
had a rasping sound in it—the voice brought back
to me Adelicia.

'Come in,' I said, 'come to the parlour;' and
going out from the kitchen I led her round to the
porch and thence to the parlour, now so little frequented, and bid her rest on the settle while I
fetched some wine.

'Oh, Betty! Betty!' she moaned, 'I want to die,
not to live; but I thought I must see you first, and
pray you to pardon me. See, my feet and gown
are wet. I was just stepping into yonder mill
stream when I thought I would see you first.
Betty! Betty! pity me and forgive me. I have had
my punishment. He turns from me with loathing.
He fled when I sickened, and a week ago, when the
surgeon said I was well, I sent for him. I thought

he would be glad—might be glad—I was alive; but oh! his look when he saw me! It will haunt me in the next world—such a look. He said, "Why did you send for me? You are not well. I dread to catch this awful disease. I will send you money to get all you need, but I—" I scarce knew what more he said; I felt dazed with my sorrow. I cried, "Edmund! Edmund!" but he had left the chamber, and the woman who had remained in the house to tend me found me in a swoon, from which she thought I should never wake. Betty, why don't you speak to me? What! sure you are not crying for me—sure you hate me?'

I was too much overcome to speak. I went and fetched the wine, and coming back, I held the cup to her lips, and made her swallow its contents.

'What shall I do? What will become of me?' she moaned.

'You can remain here. Come upstairs with me and I will put you to bed.'

'You mean that?'

'Yes; your clothes are drenched with water; you are worn out and weary. When you are rested we will talk of what it is best to do. You will catch a bad rheum if you do not get your clothes off. Come!'

I led her upstairs to a vacant chamber, of which

there were several to spare now, and undressing her I put on her one of my night sacques and laid her in the bed. Madge peeped in at the door and said,—

'Is she mad? Rhoda says she is mad, and I am afeard of mad folks.'

'Run away,' I said; but Madge still stood peering into the chamber.

'What does that child say? Does she say I am mad? Yes, yes, mad with grief and sin.'

'How ugly her face is!' Madge exclaimed; 'it's all pock-marked like Goody Mercer's husband. Faugh!'

I hustled Madge out of the room, and, feeling very angry with her, boxed her ear. She turned defiantly on me and, laughing, said,—

'You ar'n't like an angel now; you are a fury, but I don't care,' and with that she tore downstairs, and I saw her from the window flying across the pleasance to the orchard where I had often taken refuge in past days.

I had a sore time for the next few days, and had it not been for Mr Perceval I should indeed have been forlorn. He prayed by my poor step-mother every day, and did the same kind office for Adelicia. She was sick with a fever coming on so soon after smallpox, which made it doubtful whether she would live or die.

I went from one chamber of sickness and suffering to the other, and could scarce have borne the anxiety if I had not had a strong arm to rest on.

My stepmother sank to her longed-for rest on Easter Even, with words of blessing on her lips for me, and leaving me to do as I felt best for poor, wayward Madge and the disposition of the farm.

Mr Perceval insisted on Edmund Pelham being summoned, and I was therefore constrained to relate to him the sad story of his wife, who lay sick in the little upper chamber above my stepmother's.

A messenger was despatched for Edmund, and it fell to me to receive him in the porch, which, try as I would to conquer the feeling, ever reminded me of the tale of love he had told there, and of the sad sequel.

Edmund did not profess to feel any sorrow for my stepmother's death, and when I led him into the parlour, said carelessly,—

'You are mistress here now, Betty. I will help you to settle any matters which require legal advice.'

I saw he was speaking thus to avoid any reference to Adelicia, nor had he any preparation for the news of her being under the same roof.

'I have much to say to you, Edmund, about your wife, before we enter into other matters.'

'My wife? oh! poor soul, she has been near dying of smallpox. It has gone to her brain, for she has wandered in her speech, the woman who tended her tells me.'

'Your wife is here,' I said, 'under this roof.'

He shuddered visibly, as if struck by a sudden blow.

'Here!' he said. 'How does that fall out?'

'She arrived here four days ago in a piteous condition—a broken heart had led her to think of ending her sorrows in the mill stream yonder. By God's mercy that grief is spared you.'

'Poor thing!' he said, 'she is so fearfully scarred by smallpox. It may be death would be welcome.'

These hard words from the man I had once loved and trusted smote me with pain and in-dignation.

'How can you speak thus,' I said, 'of one whose happiness you have wrecked! one who was led into wrong-doing by you, and who is now lying sick, and in misery of mind and body, under this roof. For shame, Edmund! I can scarce believe you are so changed as to be hardened against your wife. Go to her and speak some words of comfort to her, and try to retrieve past coldness by kindness and sympathy.'

'I cannot—I cannot, Betty; it is too dreadful to

look on a face where not a trace of the beauty it once had is left. No, I cannot see her yet. The shock, when I went at her bidding, was too great to repeat it. I dread that pestilence which is now walking abroad, with no respect of high or low. It is loathsome, it is fearful.'

Nothing that I could say changed Edmund's determination.

He was liberal with his purse, and said if I would keep his wife, he would pay well for the care taken of her. But see her he could not and would not.

'You could never have loved Adelicia,' I said, 'for real love is not affected by any outward change of face or form.'

'That is well said on the stage or read in romances, Betty, but it will not be proved true in actual life.'

Mr Perceval went through all the business part of the affairs with Edmund, and it was settled that the farm should be kept on, and a good woman placed in the house who would look after the dairy, and be put in a position of authority over the labourers till such time as I could return to live at Ivy Farm.

This woman, Mrs Turner by name, had lately been widowed, and was thankful to find a home.

K

Mr Perceval knew her to be honest and trusty, and he it was who advised me in this as in every other matter. Madge was to be sent to board at school in Hitchin, and to return in the holidays to the farm. Poor Adelicia happily asked no questions about Edmund, and, indeed, she had scarce strength to do so. She was prostrate in mind and body, a wreck of her former self.

The funeral of my stepmother well over, and the settlements made, I was eager to return to Westminster. The apothecary said Adelicia was not now in danger of her life, and I need not stay longer on her account. I said as much to Mr Perceval, and his reply was,—

'You desire not to stay, you say, on Mistress Pelham's account. But will you not stay on mine? You know how deeply and truly I love you. The little Rectory of Barton is only waiting for your sweet presence, where, far from the turmoil of the city, we may live in peace, serving our Lord and Master. Say, Betty, will you come to me?'

'Not yet! not yet!' I pleaded; 'it is not possible for me to leave Mistress Purcell now. I must be with her for some months at least. She and the dear master have been good and true friends to me, and I cannot leave them yet.'

'You would not say this, Betty, if you were sure of your own heart; you would not say this if you could return my love.'

'I must wait, I must wait,' I said; 'do not press me yet. I am so grateful to you, so full of respect for you.'

'That will suffice,' he said hastily, 'that will suffice. One question I ask, Is there another man to whom you could readily give your heart?'

And to this I answered, with all sincerity, 'No.'

'Am I giving you pain?' I questioned, as he turned his head away to hide his emotion.

'The pain of disappointment,' he said; 'but it will pass. I will wait, I will serve, as I told you, seven years for my Rachel!'

So good and noble was his nature that he forbore to say more, nor did he urge me to marry him. I put my hand in his, after a pause, as we stood together again in the little porch, with all the freshness of the spring around us, the birds singing their evensong, and the ripple of the mill stream sounding with the drowsy tinkle of the cow-bells as they went back to pasture after the milking.

Poor Adelicia! it was hard to leave her, and I thought I should never have courage to do so. I asked her if I should say aught about her to the Chanter, her uncle, but she cried aloud at the bare notion,—

'No, no, I pray you never name me to him!' Then suddenly, 'Tell me, Betty, tell me truly, is my face less dreadful to look at than it was at first?'

I dared not be untruthful, yet I grieved to answer her as I felt I must answer her.

'I dared not look in the glass in my own house, and there is no glass in this chamber,' she said. 'Be my mirror, Betty, and tell me what you see.'

'I see the traces of the dreadful malady which spares none who have been attacked by it; but time works wonders, as in the case of a young choir boy, whom I often see at Westminster. His face has resumed its proper colour, and his eyes their brightness.'

'And mine! and mine!' she moaned. 'My eyes are dim, my face distorted; it is all purplish red, and no one would know me. I heard him murmur as much. Ah! Betty, what it was to me to see him start back and exclaim under his breath, "My God! what a spectacle!"'

'Do not give him another thought,' I said; 'he is unworthy of it. When you are recovered, he shall hear of it, and, let us hope—'

'Hope! hope! I have no hope left in me. I long, yes, I long to die.'

'Life and death, sickness and health, are in God's hands. You have yet a long life before you, and you must pray to God to help you to bear your trouble, and help you also to use the gift of preserved life for Him.'

So I left her, poor, poor Adelicia, and my heart was heavy for her. What had so changed Edmund since the days when he frequented the farm, and protested that he loved me? Was I deceived in him always? Was he never what I believed him to be? or was he changed by contact with the world? He was flattered and caressed, and had been noticed at Court, and was spoken of, Mr Purcell said, as one like to rise to the highest honours as a lawyer. His heart was hardened against his wife, and he seemed to forget all the misery he had brought on her. Yes, Edmund Pelham was changed; and as I acknowledged it to myself, while the stage rumbled on towards London, I felt the insecurity of all earthly stays and supports, and tried to rest on God.

CHAPTER VII

A.D. 1688

I RETURNED to my friends in Dean's Yard to share in the joy which the birth of a little daughter had occasioned.

She was baptised in the Abbey by the name of Frances, and, unlike her little brothers who were buried there, she was a strong, hearty child. She became a dear delight to me, and it was sweet to me to find that her parents suffered me to share their pleasure with them.

'You belong to us in joy and sorrow,' Mrs Purcell would say, 'and you must never leave us.'

It was necessary for me, when Mrs Purcell spoke thus, to tell her that Mr Perceval was my suitor, and would fain have me for his wife.

'Not yet—not yet, Betty; we cannot spare you; you must not leave us yet.'

'No,' I replied. 'I have no present wish to do so, but I felt it right to tell you that, if I wed any

man, it will be Master Perceval, unless, I added,
'he should change and no longer desire me for
his wife.'

'Well, well,' Mrs Purcell would say, 'it is right
for you to have a prospect of marriage. There
have been several of our friends who would fain
find favour in your eyes. Now they can be assured
that your hand is promised. Master Perceval is
too solemn for my taste, and I think is severe
on Susanna Mountfort for her gaiety and her
association with actors. However, the people are
now too full of apprehension to frequent the
theatres, and William Mountfort has actually given
up the stage for the time to live hard by
with the Chief Justice, who, it is said, is falling
into disfavour with the King.'

I said at the outset of the story of my life that
I had nothing that was startling in my experience
to record, but that I had been brought into contact
with other lives which were remarkable.

This month of May, which had brought joy to
my dear master and his wife, was fraught with
grave events for the Church and people of England.

I can never forget the day when one of the
prebendaries came hastily in, saying that the Declaration for giving liberty of conscience was to be
read in the Abbey by the Dean's order, but there

was scarce another church where it would be read, the feeling against it was so strong; and no wonder. It was in reality a cover for the giving the Papists full licence, and the others— dissenters and the like—were only mentioned as a make-weight.

'But,' the prebendary said, 'it is to be read in the Abbey, and there is an end of it.'

'No end,' Mr Purcell; 'this is but the beginning of trouble, you may depend on it. There is a storm brewing which will break ere long,' and he was right.

The King had been incensed when seven of the Bishops addressed him praying to be excused from ordering the Declaration to be read in their dioceses, and on the eighth day of June the Archbishop of Canterbury and six Bishops were sent to the Tower for contumacy.

Mr Perceval came to London, and presented himself in Dean's Yard, for his concern about this Declaration of the King's was very great.

He asked me to go with him to witness the disembarking of the Bishops at the Tower Wharf. I felt safe with Mr Perceval, and indeed the crowd collected was quiet and orderly. The most part were on their knees as the Bishops passed along, and prayed aloud for them, begging for their blessing.

As they passed out of sight under the dark gateway of the Tower, I ventured to ask Mr Perceval, who seemed deeply moved, whether he had read the Declaration in his church on the day appointed.

To this he answered,—

'No; nor would I read it were I commanded to do so a hundred times. Far sooner would I go with yonder good, holy men to the Tower.'

'Yet,' I said, 'tolerance is a virtue for princes to exercise.'

'Tolerance! This is scarce to be called tolerance. It will serve the King's own ends. The chief places in Church and State are filling fast with the Papists, and this declaration is but a confirmation of what we have seen at hand—the King has broken faith with the nation.'

We had much pleasant converse on our homeward way.

'In Adelicia,' Mr Perceval said, 'there is as yet no change. She refuses to be comforted, and I have given Mistress Turner strict charge to watch her narrowly lest she should escape and do violence to herself.'

He asked me if I had thought well over what he had said to me before I left Ivy Farm.

Yes, I had thought well over it, but still asked

for delay. I cannot say why I was so long holding back from one who thus honoured me with his love. Mayhap it was that the wound of betrayal would still ache and smart.

How patient he was with me; how gentle, how tender; and he proved himself then, as ever, a true-hearted and steadfast man.

Before we returned to Dean's Yard, he said he had a mind to go and find his sister at the Chancellor's, which was close at hand.

I dreaded to go to the grand house in Duke Street, and begged to be taken home, that he might go thither alone. But he said he would not spare me, and surely I was not afraid of William Mountfort? No, but of the Chancellor, he had such an eagle glance, and when I saw him at the wedding feast I shuddered when I thought of all the dreadful cruelty of his sentences on the innocent. It amazed me to think William Mountfort could be so devoted to Jeffreys; at which Mr Perceval asked me if I remembered Saul's love for David, and how the evil spirit departed from him when he played before him.

'I think this tie between the Chancellor and Will Mountfort is of the same character. He charms by his wit and humour, by his beautiful voice, and by the evenness of his temper.'

The Chancellor lived in much state, and we were ushered by lacqueys into the withdrawing-room of the stately house, where we found William Mountfort singing a song, the music composed by my dear master.

William did not stop on our entrance, and Susanna held up her hand to prevent us from interrupting.

The Chancellor lay back in a chair richly covered with crimson velvet. He beat time on the carved arms with his large yet shapely hands, the fingers loaded with rings. He did not seem to notice our entrance, and his keen eyes were fixed on the singer.

When the song ceased, the Chancellor said,—

'Well done, Will, you have chased away the phantoms for this time—ugly phantoms which are wont to visit me day and night. As I am bidden to sup with the King, I must needs be in a mood to suit his sacred Majesty. This has been a fine day's work truly; by this time their rebellious lordships are safe in the Tower, I take it.'

'Yes, my lord,' Mr Perceval said; 'we have seen them taken thither amidst the tears and prayers of the people.'

'We—we! Who are we?'

Mr Perceval had made a deep reverence to the Chancellor, while Susanna took my hand and said,—

'This is the promised bride of my brother, my lord.'

'Ha! and a winsome bride she is. I have seen her before. Is it not so, fair lady?'

'I saw your lordship at the wedding feast of Master Mountfort.'

'Ah! I remember, I remember. I have eyes for fair ladies, including Mistress Bracegirdle. Is it not so, Will?'

William Mountfort assented with a smile. I thought the smile had sadness in it.

'The fair one favours none of her admirers. Is it not so, Will?'

'She has a kind word and a smile for all her friends, and these be amongst the poorest as well as the richest,' William Mountfort replied.

'Yes,' Susanna Mountfort said, putting her hand into her husband's arm, as if to assure him of her faith in him, for rumours were afloat that Mrs Bracegirdle had an especial kindness for him. 'Yes, my lord, and this is one of her chief friends, who would defend her and her good name at the point of the sword if need arose.'

'Well spoken, well spoken, fair lady,' the Chancellor said. 'Hark ye, Will, there is no greater blessing in the world than a true and loyal wife like your Sue.'

'I am well aware of it, my lord, and well do I know I have won a prize in mine.'

The servants soon after announced that his lordship's chair was waiting, and we took our leave. As we passed out, we saw the chair, with powdered footmen in fine liveries standing ready to carry my lord to Whitehall, and a crowd collected to see him depart.

'Gilded state, indeed,' Mr Perceval said; 'but I would sooner be one of those brave bishops in the Tower than Lord Chancellor to serve a king like James.

'I have heard some folks speak of him as winning and gracious in manner, and ready to pardon offenders.'

'Ay, that may be, but there is no reliance to be placed in him, as time will show.'

Mr Perceval returned to his cure on the next day, but we saw no more of him after he left me at Mr Purcell's house. He declared his intention of seeing Edmund Pelham and reprimanding him for his cruel desertion of his wife. Whether his words had any effect we did not hear, but this I am sure, they were spoken in all sincerity, and yet gently and kindly.

It was soon after noon on the day but one following that I, sitting in the parlour with the baby Frances

in my arms, was startled by the report of guns and
the sudden clang of bells. Mr Purcell, coming in,
said,—

'The Tower ordnance are firing for the birth of a
Prince, so, my little daughter,' he went on, taking the
infant from my arms, 'you and the Prince of Wales
have entered into this troublesome life nearly at
the same time; but, sweet little Frances, I predict
thy life will be a happier one than the little
Prince's—God grant it!' Then he covered the
child with kisses, which awoke her, and she began
to whimper. 'What, am I too rough with thee,
sweet one? There, I am but an awkward nurse,
go back to thy gentler one, who tends thee with
such loving care.'

It was a time of startling events. As my dear
master said, there was scarce time to breathe after
the surprise caused by one, when another claimed
attention. Through the kindness of my dear
master I was with him in Westminster Hall when
the Bishops were brought up to hear the indictment
read. Never can I forget the sight of those seven
noble men, who stood with unshaken firmness as
the indictment was read. They were at last dis-
missed on their own recognisances for two weeks.

These weeks were weeks of ferment in many
quarters.

Those who came in to the Purcells house, and they were numerous, had all tales to tell of the growing discontent abroad.

There were whisperings that the little Prince was no prince at all; that he had been brought in a warming-pan to the Queen's chamber, and that the King connived at the deceit. And although at first many laughed at the folly of the story, it grew with the telling, and gained credence.

Mr Purcell was completing a thanksgiving anthem for the birth of the Prince, and an ode for the King quickly followed. He was ever so fully occupied with music, which was as the very air he breathed, and as the sustenance on which he depended, that the great matters occupying the thoughts of the King's subjects were not affecting him so deeply as might have been supposed. Then his delight in the healthy, happy babe who had been given him after the loss of her infant brothers was ever a wellspring of joy to him. As I sat with the babe in my arms, for her mother was but weak and frail, and could ill bear any fatigue, Mr Purcell would play softly some sweet air on the harpsichord and say, as he turned his head to gaze on the sleeping child,—

'Is that like the song of the angels, little one? Sure she smiles as she hears it.'

It was but a fancy of her father's, for little Frances only smiled as do most infants without any meaning; but the fancy pleased him, and I can see before me now his beautiful face alight with parental love and tenderness and pride.

Owing to Mrs Purcell's weakness and shrinking from being exposed to the fatigue of a long day in Westminster Hall, when the Bishops were to appear to be tried, I was witness to a scene which must ever remain as one of the most striking in the history of this kingdom.

This scene has been described by many, and yet, in recording the events of my own life, I cannot pass it over without a word, more especially as the decision in after years of those who were called Non-Jurors—that is, refused to take the oaths of allegiance to King William and Queen Mary— affected my own lot so painfully. Nay, I recall that word; there should be no pain in the participation I had in the noble protest of one I loved for honour's sake.

There was a goodly assemblage in that stately Hall of Westminster on the twenty-ninth day of June 1688—Saint Peter's Festival—which, to many, was thought a significant coincidence.

The bearing of these Bishops, with the Arch-

Westminster Hall and Abbey, from the River. Seventeenth Century.

ɔishop at their head, impressed all onlookers. There was no defiance in their mien; only a ːalm determination which was dignified and imɔressive.

Sir Samuel Astry's voice, strong and resonant, ısked if his Grace of Canterbury and their Lordɩhips of Ely, Chichester, St Asaph, Bristol, Peterɔorough and Bath and Wells pleaded guilty or ɪot guilty to the charge brought against them.

What a long day it was! The heat was all ɔut unbearable, yet none who had seats or even ɩtanding room thought of leaving their places.

It was therefore a disappointment to find, just ɩs the Abbey clock struck out six, that the jury, ɔeing unable to agree in their verdict, were to be ɔcked up till nine o'clock the next morning.

But what a great burst of rejoicing was heard ɦe next day when it was known the Bishops were ɩcquitted.

A lane of people, high and low, rich and poor, ɔn their knees, was made as the Bishops passed ɦrough, to beg their blessing. And as to the ɪight, it was like day with bonfires, and the bells of ɩvery church rang out merry peals for the righteous ɣerdict which had been obtained, despite the nightɔng resistance of the king's brewer, who was one ɔf the jurors.

L

Of all the confusion and turmoil with which the
kingdom was disturbed during the next few months,
I had no greater share than that of hearing of it
from those who came and went in Dean's Yard.

William Mountfort and Susanna, who were still
living in Lord Jeffreys' house near by, frequently
came and brought us tidings of what was passing.

William Mountfort had a sore time of it with
the Chancellor. He cursed and swore at the
vacillation of the King, well knowing that he would
fall with him, if, indeed, the Prince of Orange,
whose landing in England was daily looked for,
succeeding in wresting the Crown from him. It
was William Mountfort who gave us piteous
accounts of the King's constant change of front,
at one moment defying his enemies, at the next
shrinking before them. But, as was natural, the
condition of the poor Queen touched Mrs Purcell's
heart and mine most deeply.

Early in December the Queen was left alone at
Whitehall surrounded with spies and traitors, and
knowing not where to turn; her child was taken
from her by the King's order, and only by the
urgent entreaty of Lord Dartmouth did he consent
to have him recalled, under the care of Lord and
Lady Powis, from Portsmouth to Whitehall.

To think of the babe tossed about after this

manner,' Mrs Purcell said; 'sure, it will kill him to be exposed to the wintry weather. My heart aches for his mother.'

William Mountfort came in with startling news on the evening of the eighth day of December. He was greatly agitated, and said,—

'All is lost now; the Chancellor has surrendered the Great Seal to the King, having used it for the last time to seal the writs for a general election. He is like one distraught; he is tearing up papers and throwing aside books, venting his temper on the lacqueys, who, scenting what is in the air, sneer and openly scoff at him. I can scarce bear more of it. I have sent Susanna to her father; it is not meet for her to hear the Chancellor's language; yet I have loved him, and even now would help him if I could.'

This news of the Chancellor's fall was followed the next day by the story of the poor Queen's escape with her child. Of this, her marvellous escape, William Mountfort, by reason of his intimacy with one of the gentlemen about the Court, was a witness. This gentleman had gained knowledge of the Queen's flight, and being devoted to her and burning with indignation against those who had circulated the shameful lies as to the identity of the child, had invited William Mountfort to cross to Lambeth with him, where a coach was to be in readiness to receive her and the infant prince.

'"I should like to be assured," this gentleman said, "of my Queen's safety, and, if it be possible, let her have the assurance of my allegiance and desire to accompany her on her journey."

'This he could not do from Whitehall, for the Count de Lauzun had a grudge against him, and like as not would have worked him mischief.

'Thus I started with him before dark, paying a boatman a large fee to take us across from the horse ferry.

'A night of storm and pouring rain made even the boatman hesitate. He was bribed by a gold piece and our telling him we were bound to reach Lambeth owing to the sickness of a relative. We got safely across, though in danger of our lives from the rocking of the crazy craft.

'The evening soon closed in, and we repaired to a little hostel to refresh ourselves and dry our clothes.'

'The Queen was not to leave Whitehall till two o'clock, so we had time enough and to spare. I dozed, but my companion could not close his eyes. He walked up and down the little kitchen where we had been permitted to shelter from the raging of the wind and the ceaseless downpour of cold rain that was mixed with particles of frozen snow.

'What a night! and what a morning! I felt then,' William Mountfort said, 'how far the tragedy of real life exceeds the tragedy which we act on the stage. For this was a tragedy indeed. A gentle-nurtured Queen and her child, a Prince of royal blood, tossed on the dark waters of the river in peril of their lives, escaping from what were truly the foes of her own household.

'As soon as the clock of old Lambeth Church struck three, we left the hostel, telling the host that we must hasten, despite the rain and storm, to the sick relative we had come to see.

'He looked at us suspiciously and said, if we were a pair of evil Jesuits, he was sorry he had given us shelter, "for," says he, "as to your sick relative, I dare to say it's a pack of lies, and there are no liars like the Jesuits."

'My friend paid the man handsomely, thereby stopping his tongue, and it was a relief when we heard him bang and bolt the door behind us.'

William Mountfort had a marvellous gift for description, and it is vain for me to try to give the narrative after the forcible fashion in which he gave it to us.

There was a little concourse of listeners. Mrs Purcell with her babe clasped to her breast, several of their neighbours and friends, and old Mrs Purcell with her son Edward.

My dear master stood leaning against the back of the settle on which his wife was seated, now and again looking down on the happy infant quietly asleep, and yet listening intently to William Mountfort's story.

'The gale blew more and more fiercely,' William Mountfort said, 'the rain descended in torrents, and bitter was the cold. My friend and I—he bade me keep back his name by reason of the prejudice against him in certain quarters, he being a Protestant—heard a voice calling aloud for Dusiores.

'"The page of the backstairs," my companion whispered, "let us draw nearer the bank under cover of the darkness."

'"No coach waiting, curse you!" we heard a muffled voice say.

'"No," said another, "but it will be here anon."

'Then, guided by a single torch, which smoked in the rain and gave but a weird light, we saw the figure of Her Majesty withdraw to the shelter of the walls of old Lambeth Church.

'We crept round, and the projecting side of the porch in which the Queen stood saved us from observation. Indeed, in the blackness of darkness this was not difficult to escape. We were so near we heard the Queen's agonised murmur,—

'"If he wakes, oh, my God! if he should wake and cry, he will betray us. Holy Mary, have pity, have pity, and send the chariot which is to take us out of danger."

'Long, long did she wait, and it seemed an eternity to her and to the little company who had cast in their fortunes with her.

'My friend drew nearer to the spot where the Queen stood. I heard him murmur,—

'"God save your Majesty and the Prince. I am ready to die for you."

'What the answer was I cannot tell, but it must have been a gracious one.

'The coach came swiftly up at this moment. There was a movement in the little company, then the torch flared up, and for an instant I saw the face of the Queen, her babe clasped to her breast, then the sound of the coach door as it was closed, and I found myself alone. Whether my friend had climbed on the back of the coach I know not. This is my story, for I saw him no more.

'There was no sound now but the rush of the river and the swirl of the water against the posts where the boat was moored which had brought over the Queen.

'A dim light at the prow guided me to it, and, waiting for no permission, I jumped in, hoping my friend might be there. But I was alone with the boatmen, who rowed hard against wind and tide, not noticing my presence till we landed at the horse ferry.

'"What do you here?" they asked, with an oath.

'"I wanted to cross the river," I said, tossing the ruffian a piece of silver, and then I was right glad to find myself ashore, making my way as speedily as might be to Duke Street, where I found, as I say, all things in a hubbub, and those who had cringed before the Chancellor, and flattered him, leaving him to his fate.'

William Mountfort left us for that time, to return the next day with the further news that the King had fled, and had thrown the Great Seal into the Thames, and that the Chancellor had fled, like his master, and, disguised as a common sailor, hoped to escape beyond the seas.

I remember to this day, and it strikes me more forcibly now that I look back on it than at the time when all these events were taking place, that Mr Purcell was undisturbed in the midst of storm —following his business with unabated diligence and composing music, which sure will be sung when the great revolution of that year will have passed into dim remembrance.

At matins and evensong, at the Abbey, whither, to quiet our troubled spirits, Mrs Purcell and I resorted by turns, the music my dear master drew forth from the organ was, sure, never more beautiful.

He had always a composition on hand, always some music floating in his brain, always living in the delight its expression gave him, never satisfied with what he achieved, ever longing to do something better and higher.

Within the walls of the house in Dean's Yard there was peace. Love struck the chords, and the harmony was scarce ever disturbed by a false note. I dare scarce trust myself to write more of my dear master, as I saw him day by day; and I can hear his voice now as he crooned snatches of melody over his babe Frances, when, as sometimes happened, she was fractious with the ailments of infancy. Her father seldom failed to soothe her, and she would lift her tiny fingers and stroke his face or play with the lace of his cravat, and smile on him through the tears which were but as an April shower, and, quick to come, were quick to pass.

This fateful year closed in gloom and sadness for the nation, although there were high hopes set on William, Prince of Orange, to whom many swore allegiance, and looked on him as a deliverer.

It may be these were right, and the country was saved by his hand from the hated thraldom of the Pope, from which the Reformation had set the people of England free. Yet there were those who, like myself and Mrs Purcell, could weep to think of the exiled King, whose heart-broken cry when he heard of his daughter's desertion gave sorrow to many a heart.

'God help me!' he said, 'even my own children have forsook me.'

BOOK IV

1689

'A man that I love, and honour with my soul, and my heart, and my duty, and my life, and my being, and my uttermost power.'—SHAKESPEARE (*Henry V.* Act III.)

CHAPTER VIII

A.D. 1689

THE Coronation of the new King and Queen Mary in Westminster Abbey was the occasion of some trouble in our little household, which is perhaps too important for me to pass over.

Mr Purcell believed he had full command of the organ loft at the north side of the choir, where a fine view of the ceremony was obtained. And for my part, though my opinion may not be worth the hearing, I think there was justice in the claim.

Whether or not it was right to take money for the places I cannot decide, though, if it had been done before, sure Mr Purcell was not so greatly to blame if he followed old usage.

Those who have read my story up to this point may remember that I did not witness the grandeur which marked the Coronation of King James. Therefore I was pleased to be told I was to accompany Mrs Purcell to the loft and that Mr Purcell's mother would keep the house and tend baby Frances on that day.

We were all astir early. My dear master trying the effect of 'the anthem which he had composed in honour of the event, at break of day, on the small chamber organ which he had lately placed in one of the parlours where rehearsals took place, was enough to chase away our slumbers.

Mr Purcell had bidden some of his friends to accompany us early that we might get the first places in the loft.

Amongst those who arrived in Dean's Yard in the spring dawning were Mrs Bracegirdle and William and Susanna Mountfort, with Edmund Pelham, who had the escort of two gay ladies in bright attire.

We all assembled in the parlour, where, by Mrs Purcell's order, cups of wine and cakes were handed round by me.

Edmund Pelham was not behind anyone in the richness of his dress. He was full of merriment, and bandied jokes with William Mountfort. He greeted me as one he knew well, and maybe liked, but with no particular expression of pleasure in seeing me.

When I had handed him the wine cup and the platter of cakes, I said,—

'Tidings were brought me yesterday from Mistress Pelham.'

'Ah! poor soul! Is she recovering?'

My heart burned with indignation as I answered,—

'Recovered in health but not in mind. When will it please you to take her home?'

One of the gay ladies, whom he called Mistress Cynthia, now said,—

'I never heard say you had a mother, Master Pelham. What has ailed her?'

I waited a moment, sure Edmund would speak, but he pretended to be engaged with answering Mrs Purcell's question as to whether he had been well served. I could not help it. I replied for him,—

'Master Pelham's wife, madam, has been sorely stricken with smallpox.'

'Ah!' Mistress Cynthia screamed, 'has he been nigh her? Is there fear of catching it?'

'You need have no fears on that score,' I said. 'Master Pelham has not seen his wife for some months.'

Edmund Pelham was a master in the art of concealment. He now turned with a smile, saying,—

'It must be time to be departing for the Abbey.

Shall I have the honour of conducting you thither,
fair ladies? Mistress Bracegirdle is well provided
for,' he added, with a laugh.

William Mountfort was indeed in earnest consultation with Mrs Bracegirdle, who was evidently
urging on him some request. I heard the last
few words,—

'I pray you be cautious; he is a tiger in cruelty
and a serpent in guile, with which last he gains
his ends. Oh! I pray you, beware!'

William Mountfort took her hand and kissed it,
and I knew no more, but I noticed that Susanna
Mountfort put her hand caressingly into Mrs
Bracegirdle's arm, and there was the utmost
cordiality subsisting between them.

We were now ready to start for the Abbey.
The light was still dim, for the morning was dark
and rain threatened; the link-boys were still
running with their torches.

A great crowd had gathered before the west
front of the Abbey, but we entered by the
cloister door to our places.

To those who had witnessed the Coronation of King
James this seemed far less magnificent; yet to me
it was a sight that filled me with strong emotion.
The Queen had great beauty, and she bore herself with
much dignity. Yet sure there must have been sad-

ness in her heart, as she thought of her father obliged
to take flight from his country, and her infant brother
driven away with his mother from his home and
his lawful inheritance.

By the Queen's side the King looked puny and
small; his face was sallow and hard featured, and
he went through the whole ceremony as if he were
doing somewhat of a penance.

The organ loft was filled with people, and amongst
them were many who talked freely of the causes of
the change which had come about without blood-
shed, and had been to some unexpected, to others
but the natural consequences of the attitude of
King James against the Church which he had
sworn to protect with her services and ritual.

Instead, the priests and emissaries of Rome were
everywhere. As in the case of Magdalen College,
Oxford, unlawful means were used to turn out
those who held office in the Reformed Church, and
replace them with Romish priests. Mass was publicly
said in the Royal Chapels, and by subtle but
certain means Rome had been like to assert her
supremacy.

There was no Archbishop to place the crown
on King William's head. The Bishop of London
took his place. Many of the chief of the peers and
peeresses of the realm were absent, and there were

M

but five bishops and four judges. None others had taken the oath of allegiance to the new sovereigns.

A voice near me said,—

'There's news that King James is landed in Ireland, hence time-servers do well to keep away.'

'Ay,' said another, 'what if the tide turn and flow as quick as it ebbed. In a pretty condition those who are assisting here to-day would find themselves.'

Soon my whole attention was fastened on the scene below, and I leaned forward in breathless attention. The King was attended by the Bishop of London, the Queen by the Bishop of St Asaph. The Holy Bible was given to the King and Queen to kiss, and then the Bishop of Salisbury preached a long sermon. No one in the loft seemed to care to listen to his discourse, and much unseemly whispering and titters of laughter went on, such scant reverence was shown for the place where we were assembled.

For my part, I was wholly taken up by the reading of the coronation oath, both King and Queen blending their voices in assent and, each holding up the right hand, kissed the book together.

The King seemed bowed down with the weight of his grand velvet robes, with their ermine border, but the Queen carried herself from first to last with grace and dignity. There was a wondrous charm about Queen Mary, and it was the more remarkable that so gentle and gracious a lady should harden her heart against her own father, and lend credence to the foolish story of her brother's birth being fictitious. After the Coronation there was an immense crowd in Westminster Hall to witness the dining in public of the new Sovereigns. Scaffolds were erected which took up one side of the Hall. There was the usual ceremony, after the feast, of the champion riding in and throwing down a glove to challenge all who denied the right of the new Sovereigns to the throne. It is said this ceremony was for a long time delayed, and that the Queen's face betrayed great anxiety. The King's face never betrayed aught, either of fear, love, or hate—it was always, as it were, a sealed book.

I was glad to go back to the quiet of our house in Dean's Yard, but Mrs Purcell went, with others, under care of her husband, to witness the proceedings in Westminster Hall. I found Leonard Perceval awaiting my return, to my great surprise. I could not conceal my joy, and all my coldness towards him vanished.

I sprang towards him, exclaiming, 'I am glad you are come,' nor did I withdraw from his embrace as I had often done before.

'Is my sweetheart indeed glad to see me?

'Ah! yes,' I said, 'for I am weary and long for quiet. Were you present at the Coronation?' I asked.

'No, nor did I desire to be present. This assumption of the crown by William, Prince of Orange, causes grave uneasiness in many hearts, and it will affect me even in my humble position.

' How so?' I asked.

' I shall never find myself able to take the oaths of allegiance as a member of the Church is bound to take them, and thus I shall not be competent to hold the cure of Barton. I have come to London expressly to take counsel with the Bishop of Bath and Wells, and from him learn if his Grace the Archbishop, under whose jurisdiction and in whose province I hold my cure, is like to yield, or change the line of conduct he has chosen. Of this there is not the remotest chance. I have seen his chaplain and learned from him that his Grace, with the Bishops, who went with him to the Tower on the question of the Declaration, will not acknowledge the Prince of Orange as King. This,' he added, ' my sweet one, will affect my future so seriously that I cannot ask you to cast in your lot with mine.'

Now there was ever in me a strange kindling of affection for anyone who was in any sort of trouble. Thus I now knew, what I had scarcely known of a surety before, that I loved Leonard Perceval, and that whensoever he wished to make me his wife, I would be ready.

'I said,' he continued, 'I would serve seven years for my Rachel, and it may be now it will be twice seven.'

'Why should it?' I asked, and then, hiding my face on his shoulder, I said, 'I am ready to come to you. Have I not enough for both. We can live at Ivy Farm, and you can minister to the poor at Hertsby—a neglected parish scarce ever visited by the Rector, save now and again on the festivals of the Church. You can find work there.'

'Ah!' he said, stroking my hair back from my forehead, and kissing it, 'ah, my dear one, you are full of generous intentions, but I must pause ere I take advantage of your goodness.'

'Now I will hear naught in that strain,' I said; 'I am yours henceforth, to do as you bid me, and to be true to you while I live.'

My change of mood, for I had never been thus free to tell him what was in my heart before— though I now knew this love had been hidden there for a long space—seemed to surprise him.

For an instant I questioned whether he thought me wanting in maidenly reserve in making this confession—only for an instant, for struggling with what was evidently strong emotion, Leonard said,—

'I came hither thinking I was the bearer of news which might decide my fate, and that you would

not care to share the lot of a houseless and home-
less minister of the Church, who will surely be
deprived of his living. Instead, this news has been
a blessing in disguise, for it has shown me the
treasure of your love is mine, which before I had
sometimes questioned. Thank God! thank God!
that question is for ever set at rest.'

So in the little parlour of Mr Purcell's house
—while the immense throng outside Westminster
Hall was shouting huzzas for the new King and
Queen, while the great events of the revolution and
change of Sovereigns, of the news from Ireland,
spreading rapidly, that King James was raising
troops and was determined to fight against those
who had conspired to take away his crown—we
two, small and of no repute, were forgetting everything in the sweet consciousness of our mutual
love.

Yes, I can say with all my heart, that from that
hour my life was illuminated by the sunshine of
Leonard's love, and all changes and chances and
sorrows which befell me were as naught; light as
dust in the balance when weighed with it.

Leonard told me that Adelicia was still distressed
and troubled by the condition of her face — that
she had tried some lotions made by a travelling
quack, who went about the country selling his wares,

potions and draughts, which he made believe were certain cures for every disease. His lotion had increased, instead of lessening, the evil, and the marks left by the smallpox were worse rather than better for this man's prescription.

' It is vain for Mistress Turner to tell her that time is the only cure for the mischief wrought by that terrible scourge, and that it does often soften the hard lines and reduce the red blotches in size. She will not listen and is by times peevish and fretful, or moody and sullen. A piteous sight. I think of making an appeal to Pelham to ease her poor heart of its burden, but I fear me it will be in vain.'

Leonard told me Madge had been tamed by school discipline, and that of the two boys aboard ship good reports had been sent through Mr Gostling. But, to say truth, we soon left the affairs of others to recur to our own.

He would not stay to sup; but before he left me he put on my finger a ring which had been his mother's, with this posy, ' Together heavenwards.'

He said he had kept it in his purse for a long time, with the design of putting it on my finger as a sign of betrothal, but that he had never felt sure of my love till this blessed day, which, said he, will mark the Coronation of William and Mary, the so-called King and Queen, for ever in my calendar with a red letter.

And so he left me in a happy dream of bliss, from which I was roused by the return of Mrs Purcell.

She was faint and weary with the day's long spectacle, and asked in an irritated voice for her child.

'She is with her grandmother,' I said, 'who, when she has her in charge, does not brook any interference.'

'That is a pretty excuse. I thought to find her in your arms. You know full well grandmother is apt to be cross if the blessed angel cries. I must climb the stairs to find out how it fares with my sweet babe, though I have scarce a breath to draw or a leg to stand on.'

And, overwrought and tired, Mrs Purcell fell a-weeping, and I had much ado to make her take some cordial and lie down on the settle.

'You look pleased enow,' she said presently. 'What has come over you, Betty?'

I showed my finger with the ring, in which a large blue sapphire shone.

'What does it mean? What does it mean?'

'That I have promised to be Leonard Perceval's wife whensoever he pleases.'

'And leave me—leave me now I need you so sorely. Oh, how cruel! how graceless!'

And again there was a burst of tears and sobs.

'Nay, dear mistress,' I said; 'I will not leave you till after your babe's birth.'

'You promise; you vow you will not?'

'Yes,' I said, 'I do.'

She quieted down then, and I went to the upper chamber to ask old Mrs Purcell to take the babe to her mother, as she was too weary to climb the steep stairs.

'And no wonder, after gadding about since daybreak. She goes the road to kill herself. My poor son is burdened with a wife who is always ailing.'

'Shall I take little Frances to her mother?'

'No; you had best see to the preparation of supper. My son will come home faint and hungry.' The baby opened her eyes, and, seeing me, held out her arms with a whimper to come to me. 'Take her, then,' her grandmother said; 'sure I've had enough of her company this day—and what a hubbub there is still going on,' for the noise of huzzas and the glare in the sky of the fireworks which were let off in every quarter made the night almost like the day.

I carried the babe to her mother, and by her presence all rough places were smoothed down.

Mrs Purcell called me to kneel by her side as the child lay in her arms, telling me she was glad

I was to be the wife of a good man like Mr Perceval, and that she would not be selfish, but when the time came would give me a wedding feast 'as fine as I shall give to my little Frances when she is wedded.'

We waited long for the master's return; and, worn out with the day's fatigue, I begged Mrs Purcell to retire to rest, and said that I would watch for Mr Purcell to come home.

' I wish he would not stay out so late,' Mrs Purcell said. 'He is often complaining of his throat, and naught is worse for it than the chill night air.'

When both his wife and mother had yielded to my entreaties, and I was left alone, I sat for some time listening for the chimes of the Abbey clock as they struck the quarters, and at last midnight sounded in twelve sonorous strokes.

It was just then that I heard the dear master's step, and hastened to admit him at the door. He passed me without a word, which was so unusual with him that I feared something was amiss.

'Where is my wife?' he asked. 'Where is my mother?'

'They are both abed,' I replied; 'the day has been a tiring one.'

'Ay, you may well say that,' and Mr Purcell flung himself on the settle, saying, 'Give me a hot posset, Betty, for I am chilled in mind and body.'

I asked no questions. I have always found that questions are only an irritation when there is some trouble pressing on one who does not show any desire of confiding in me, what that trouble is.

'This has been a pretty day's work for me, Betty.'

'A tiring day's work.'

'Ah, worse! The Chanter called me aside in the vestibule this afternoon, and asked by whose permission the organ loft was filled with gay folk, and by whom they were bidden to sit there. I answered by me, and I believed I had a right to bid them to the organ loft. Then he asked if I took money for the place, and I said yes, and he turned away frowning, saying, I must be summoned before Dean and Chapter to make justification for my conduct if I could. Then another of the Chapter came bustling up to me, saying it was a shame that I should take money thus, and it would be for the Chapter to suspend me from my post of organist unless I could deny the charge.'

I was greatly grieved to see my dear master's evident concern.

'Say naught of this, Betty, till the summons

comes; it will be a cruel blow for my poor Fan in her present state, and I would fain spare her the pain as long as I dare do so.'

Then after he had drunk the posset his spirit seemed to revive.

'Hark, Betty, to what I say. They may take away from me the organ; they may punish me by so doing, but no Dean and Chapter, thank Heaven! can deprive me of music. It is mine and gives me a joy yonder prebendaries, and Dean at their head, know naught of. I can yet earn bread for my wife and children by my office of copyist, in which you are a help, and I am beset with applications for the setting of verses to fitting music. No, no, I will not lose heart.'

'Is it your due, this money for seats in the loft, sir?' I ventured to ask.

'It is the perquisite of the office of organist. I will hold to my rights, for my own sake and that of those who may come after me. A paltry salary such as mine may well look for augmentation by these means. Now, go to rest, child, the whole affair may blow over, and so mind and keep silence till I give you leave to speak.'

I did my dear master's bidding, but I had not long to wait for making his trouble known.

The man known as Clerk to the Chapter, Mr

Needham, arrived the following day and served Mr Purcell with a summons to attend before them on the eighteenth day of April to answer certain charges as to appropriation of moneys which were the dues of the Dean and Prebendaries of Westminster Abbey.

I took the bold resolution of seeing Mr Crespion, and begging him to deal leniently with my dear master. I had long desired to see him on another account, hoping to move him to compassion about poor Adelicia, and to beg him to use his influence to persuade her husband to take her home.

As it may be remembered, long before this time I had been summoned by the Chanter to his house when Adelicia had rebelled against his authority in the matter of her marriage, but my knees shook and my heart beat so that I could scarce speak a word when I was ushered into the Chanter's presence. Mr Crespion eyed me in anything but a pleasing manner. He waved his hand, saying,—

'Be seated, Mistress Lockwood, and let me hear your errand.'

'I came, unknown to Master Purcell, or, indeed, to anyone living, to beg you, sir, to withdraw the accusation made against my dear master.'

'Tut, tut! this is impertinence. I cannot listen to it. Master Purcell has been guilty of taking undue advantage of his position at the late Coronation of their Majesties, and he will have to refund the money he has taken, or be removed from his place as organist.'

'Sir,' I said, 'Master Purcell has the precedent in the conduct of those who have gone before him.'

'Has he? Then the sooner such conduct is condemned and stopped, the better. You are young and ignorant, Mistress Lockwood, or you would see that Master Purcell had acted unfairly, I am loth to say dishonestly.'

'He is incapable of dishonesty, sir,' I said; 'if he has done wrong, it is unwittingly. Mistress Purcell is in a frail state of health. This blow falls heavily on her, and I pray you to consider the circumstances.'

'I have considered them, and however I may lament the consequences of Master Purcell's act falling on his respected lady, this must not blind me to the fact that he is greatly to blame—very greatly to blame,' Mr Crespion said, opening a massive, silver snuff-box, and holding a pinch thoughtfully between his thumb and forefinger, while he made a movement as if to show me that my interview was at an end.

But having gone so far, though all, I felt, was to but little purpose, I determined to proceed.

'Have you heard, sir,' I asked, 'of the lamentable condition in which Mistress Pelham is placed?'

'Mistress Pelham,' the Chanter said, shutting the snuff-box with a sharp click. 'And who may she be?'

'Your niece, sir—Adelicia.'

'By heaven! Mistress Lockwood, your zeal out-runs your discretion, or rather your propriety. That name is never mentioned in my presence. I dis-owned my step-niece for misconduct, nor do I choose ever to set eyes on her again.'

'If you did, sir,' I said, my courage rising, 'you would be shocked to see her. Smallpox has de-stroyed her beauty, and she is but a wreck of her former self.'

'Let her husband see to her.'

'Ah! sir, here is the saddest part of her punish-ment. He refuses to see her, or to give her the shelter of his house. It so happens that a farm on the borders of Hertfordshire belongs to me, and Mistress Pelham is there at this time, but her heart is breaking through the desertion of her husband, and I am so bold as to ask you if you could admonish him, and show him it is his bounden duty to protect and nourish his wife.'

'You must find someone else for this office. I hear of Master Pelham as well to do, and thought of as

a keen-sighted gentleman at the Bar, though it may
be Jeffreys has dragged him down with him in his fall.
My dear Mistress Lockwood, you show youth and
ignorance of the world by your appeal. I will not
resent what many would deem an impertinence on
that score; but I must hasten to the Abbey for
matins, and you must consider our interview at an
end.'

There was naught left for me but to curtsey and
depart; but I ventured one word more,—

'May I pray you, sir, to acquit my dear master,
Master Purcell, of any dishonesty in what has
passed? What has been done has been done by
others before him. Do not, I beseech you, let him
suffer when his predecessors have gone free.'

Mr Crespion made no answer to this; and, with
cheeks aflame and tears starting from my eyes, I
returned whence I came, smarting under a sense of
defeat, which is ever a sore smart.

The next few days were days of trial and anxiety.
Many of Mr Purcell's friends rallied round him when
the matter was spread abroad. All were full of sympathy and indignation at the harsh treatment Mr
Purcell had met with at the hands of the Chapter,
for they were obdurate, and for some time we knew
not what would be the issue of the conflict.

The suspense was very hard to bear, and the quick

following of public events did not divert us from the matter which was of all importance to us in Mr Purcell's house.

He was a marvel of cheerfulness, and went on composing and playing on the organ more divinely than I had ever heard him.

William Mountfort was very frequently at the house in Dean's Yard, making plans for Mr Purcell to compose music for plays, and this took him away from us more than Mrs Purcell desired.

She had conceived a notion that the theatrical folk were not good companions for Mr Purcell, and that he frequented the places where they met too often.

But of this I can testify, that purity of life and conduct were notable in Mr Purcell from the day I entered his house, a child in years, and scarce knowing what office I was to fill in it, till that St Cecilia's day when I parted from him for ever.

Amongst those who came to Dean's Yard at this this time was Mrs Bracegirdle, who had awoke in my heart, when I first saw her, the most intense admiration.

It was beautiful to see her cast aside her cloak and hood, and seat herself on the floor with baby Frances on her knees, singing to her and toying with her

N

with all that grace of motion for which she was remarkable.

I was alone with her one summer evening, when she suddenly held the child towards me, saying,—

'Take her! take her, Betty! Would to God I were a little child again, as guileless and unharmed by contact with this miserable world.' And then the admired actress, whose fame was spreading near and far, covered her face with her hands and cried bitterly.

The mood passed, and, starting up, she said,—

'Tell me of yourself, little Betty. Susanna Mount-fort says her brother is waiting to wed you, and you put him off week after week. Do not put him off too often, or the colour of yon sapphire on your finger will fade, and love will wane.'

'Nay,' I said, 'I am too sure of Leonard's love to think of any change. I am bound to stay with those who first taught me what *home* meant, till the clouds have passed from their sky.'

'You mean as to the organist's place in the Abbey. Do you think that those worthy dignitaries would be such fools as to lose the greatest musician of the time on this quibble? Not they, not they! But I think these Non-Jurors are a riddle. Susanna says that she and her father have done their utmost to make Leonard take the oaths to the King and

Queen. He will be deprived of the cure of Burton
if he holds out — and then what? "What God
pleases," he says. Pshaw! I have no patience with
such folly; and here are these Bishops leading on
the inferior clergy to follow in their steps Sent to
the Tower by King James one day for conscience
sake, and now refusing to swear allegiance to his
successor, forsooth — also for conscience sake. I
could laugh to think of it!'

'Nay, dear madam,' I said, 'it is not a thing to be
lightly spoken of. It is a mighty grave matter, and
is causing many a good man sorrow of heart as it
causes Leonard Percival.'

'Ah! well, I do not comprehend it.'

Then she took my hand in hers—the babe having
played with it and dulled the stone in my ring with
her breath.

'See, see, the sapphire is clouded! Did I not warn
you that if it happened it would be a sign and token
of love's brightness being clouded.'

I rubbed the stone bright again with a corner of
the babe's gown, and laughing, said,—

'It is only a passing cloud—if there is one at all,
which I doubt.'

'Well,' Mrs Bracegirdle said, 'you are well out of
some one's love I could name. Edmund Pelham is a
sad rake, and that is why he will not have his wife

home to his house. He is a great favourite with the
nobles and grand folk, and those in high places, but
it will not last—pride will have a fall. How is that
poor creature, his wife? I heard she was gone
melancholy mad.'

'She is in a grievous state of mind and body,' I
said. 'She has increased the terrible redness and
scars on her face by the lotions of a pedlar in
such wares.'

'Poor creature! it must be a bitter trial to see
one's fair face so disfigured. Tell me, Betty, tell
me what man's love would last in such a case!'

'A good man's,' I replied, 'whose love was not
skin deep.'

'Ah! we have yet to prove that. I dread smallpox and death. Oh! how I dread death, and I go
through the real thing as poor, mad Ophelia and
Desdemona. As I die—when I am sweet and pure
Desdemona—I shudder and tremble, and yet I say
better death than life with a man who has lost
faith in me.'

How beautiful was Mrs Bracegirdle when she
spoke thus. Her eyes were as orbs of light, across
which the shadow of her great emotions passed like
clouds, making their exceeding brilliance more
brilliant when they shone out again. Eyes they
were that were dim with sorrow for the poor and

sad, ay, and the sin-struck, of Clare Market; eyes that often shed tears of divinest pity as she walked unscathed amidst a throng of outcasts, where others did not dare to tread, with blessings as she went. If the beauty and wondrous gifts of this fair woman worked sorrow and, as in one dire case, death for those who loved her, sure the blessings poured on her by the miserable folk of Clare Market, and the gratitude they showed for her manifold deeds of charity, may be set against these, and her name may be held, as I hold it, in reverence and affection.

And here I must quickly pass over the months that followed, and record the happy healing of the breach between the Chapter of Westminster and their organist, whose little son Edward was baptised in the Abbey by the Chanter on the seventh day of September, and I was married on the following morning to Leonard Perceval. Of my blissful life with him I will take a short survey in the next book before I write more concerning the dear master under whose roof I, as Elizabeth Lockwood, lived for five years.

BOOK V

1689—1692

My heart is great ; but it must break with silence
Ere it be disburdened with a liberal tongue.
Richard II., Act II.

CHAPTER IX

A. D. 1689

BURTON Rectory was scarce two miles from Ivy Farm, and here my husband took me one quiet autumn evening of this year.

It was a house with many gables, and the aspect was homelike, and, in my eyes, fairer than any palace could be.

As I crossed the threshold, Leonard bid me look at a motto which was carved in bold letters over the open hearth : 'Pax intrantibus, salus exeuntibus.'

'May the first be thine, sweet heart,' he said, 'and the last proved when it comes to going forth, as go we surely must.'

'Go?' I asked—'whither?'

'Whither God's hand leads us,' he said; 'but I will not cloud your home-coming by sadness. It is my home for the present time, and the future is, as I say, in God's hand.'

I was so happy in the present, the calm and

repose of the country was so sweet after the town, that I cast aside all forebodings of coming change.

'If I have you,' I said to Leonard, 'that is enough. You make my home now.'

'I shall see and consult with the good and holy Bishop of Bath and Wells before I finally decide my course; meantime, take a survey of your new home, and I will look into matters about the parish. Here is my good servant, Joyce, who will show you the upper chambers.'

Joyce was a gentle-spoken woman, who looked at me with kindly eyes.

'Sure,' she said, 'you are welcome here. His reverence has need of a wife, for it has been lonesome for him, though he is always about in the village, tending the sick and praying by them, and he has made almost daily walks to Ivy Farm, where a poor creature is in a terrible plight.'

'Yes,' I said, 'I know her history, and early on the morrow I must seek her out.'

'I am not one of these parts,' Joyce said; 'I only came hither from Canterbury, at his reverence's wish, to make the place meet for his lady. I hope you'll be satisfied. His reverence has lived in two small rooms—a parlour and bedchamber adjoining; now he will use, it's to be hoped, these large parlours.'

And Joyce threw open the door on the right side
of the hall, and I exclaimed,—

'Oh! what a lovely parlour, and another room
beyond opening from it!'

'I am glad you are pleased. Now you must come
upstairs.'

The chambers there were light and pleasant.
Yes—and the sense of home was everywhere.

Then I must needs go out and see the church.
I had often worshipped there, and it was within these
walls my husband's voice had first awoke in me the
yearning after a more excellent way than I had ever
known.

The door was open, and, passing in, I saw Leonard
kneeling on the steps before the altar, with his head
bowed in his hands. I feared to disturb him, but
I crept slowly up to him, and knelt by his
side.

The evening was closing in, and there was the
hush of autumnal stillness in the air—that stillness
which is so different from the innumerable sounds
of stir and awakening which we hear in spring.

It was a solemn eventide when, hand-in-hand,
Leonard and I passed out of the church to our
home close by.

In the western light I saw my husband's face.
It was raised to the sky above, where the evening

star hung like a silver lamp. On his face was the
look of one who had put on his armour, and was
pledged to fight against evil and wrong, and to
obey the voice of conscience at whatever cost.

'Dear heart,' he said, 'it will go hard with me to
bring you to this peaceful home only to leave it,
but the decision of the Archbishop and Bishops
is naught to me now. Whatever course they
follow, my duty is clear. I cannot take the oaths
to the new King and Queen, and my deprivation
will of necessity follow, and my place here will be
filled by a man who can swear allegiance to a
usurper.'

Having said as much, Leonard seemed to cast off
care and was cheerful and even gay as he led me to
his room lined with books, where Joyce had kindled
a bright wood fire and laid supper on the board.
Later, the man who worked on the glebe and kept
the pleasance in order, by the help of a boy, was
summoned in to prayer with Joyce. They made me
a low reverence and asked leave to bid me welcome.

'May your ladyship spend many years here,' Sam
said, 'and have health and happiness.'

Such was my first evening in my new home, and
I determined to enjoy it while I had it.

I was early at Ivy Farm on the next day. All
outward things there were prosperous—it had been

a fine harvest, and all the crops had given a good yield. But in poor Adelicia there was no change for the better. Good Mrs Turner told me she had seemingly given up hope of any recovery of her beauty, or indeed of health. She was now but a skeleton, and neither ate nor drank nor slept, often wandering about the house at night, and moaning and sobbing till it was heart-breaking to hear her.

'She is always saying she is going to seek her husband, but she has scarce the strength of a fly,' Mrs Turner said, 'and she totters when she walks.'

I was determined that Edmund Pelham should see her. I felt that he should not in justice be spared the sight which might well move the stoutest heart to pity.

On my return to the Rectory, after trying in vain to soothe and console Adelicia, I wrote a letter in strong terms to Edmund Pelham, telling him I believed his wife was dying, and imploring him to come to her. I despatched my letter by the stage, marked 'Haste—post haste and urgent' on the cover—and I also wrote to my dear master, begging him to tell the Chanter of Adelicia's condition.

Leonard saw the doctor who travelled through the district, and he told him that the nostrums and lotions Adelicia had taken from the pedlar had destroyed all chance of recovery. Indeed, St Antony's fire had set in on her poor face, and it would most like prove fatal.

Again it was my lot to watch by the suffering and dying in my old home.

Day by day Adelicia slowly but surely declined. As the end drew near, her face, in a manner extraordinary, but, as I have heard, not uncommon, cleared of its terrible humour, and the swelling and distortion vanished.

I was about to bid her good-night and run with a sense of gladness to my home, when I heard steps coming along the garden path.

'It is Edmund!' Adelicia cried. 'It is my husband! Oh! Betty, I dare not see him. I dare not let him see me.'

I had scarce time to assure her that she had regained much of her former looks when Mrs Turner came to the chamber door.

'A gentleman desires to see you, Mrs Perceval,' she said.

I bid her take my place by the bed, and I went down to meet Edmund.

Long, long ago, all feeling even of friendship for him was lost to me, but I now felt deep pity for him, a pity which had almost conquered the indignation which his treatment of Adelicia had roused in me.

I am come at your bidding, Mistress Perceval,'
he said. 'What news have you for me?'

Your wife still lives, and you may thank God
for His mercy that you are in time to receive her
pardon, little as you merit it.'

'You deal hardly with me,' he said.

'Rather, justly,' I replied; 'first, you inveigled
Adelicia into a secret marriage, then, when she fell
a victim to this dire disease, you desert her; you turn
from her with loathing, you break her heart, for with
all her faults she loved you, Edmund, and loves you
still.'

He did not speak, but stood convicted before
me, without a word of self-defence. Presently I
said,—

'I will take you to her; you must follow me.'
He shrank back, and seemed as if he were about
to refuse. 'Are you such a craven as to fear to hear
your poor wife say she forgives you, Edmund?'

'She will reproach me; she had ever a sharp
tongue. I cannot face reproaches.'

'Which, you know full well, you deserve,' I said.

'She has wanted for nothing,' he said. 'I have
sent money; I have offered to pay physicians. She
has wanted for nothing.'

She has wanted love—your love,' I said, 'and
you have basely deserted her.'

'Betty,' he said, trying to take my hand with all his old, winsome manner, 'nay, Betty, do not be so cruel to me. Once you loved me—'

'Hold!' I said. 'Not a word more of this sort. I am the proud and happy wife of a good, noble-hearted man, and the past to which you dare to refer now fills me with naught but thankfulness that I was delivered from the man who can desert his wife in the time of trouble. Now, follow me.'

An angry light shone in Edmund's eyes, but he obeyed me. I opened the chamber door and said,—

'Adelicia, your husband is here.'

Poor soul! Poor, deeply-tried soul! She raised herself in her bed, and held out her wasted arms to him with a low cry as of a creature in pain. I beckoned Mrs Turner to leave the room, and, closing the door, left the husband and wife together. It had been a great effort to me to meet and speak as I did to Edmund. I felt I could bear no more, and I ran out of the house and across the fields in the gathering twilight to my home—my blessed home—where my husband awaited me, and I threw myself sobbing into his arms, to be comforted and soothed by his tender words.

Edmund remained at Ivy Farm, and was with his wife till she died. I saw her only once after that first night of Edmund's arrival. She seemed comforted by his presence, and told me, with tears running down her face, that he said she looked more like herself, and that she would get better and live.

'But I do not wish to live,' she said. 'He will soon find another wife, and it is better I should die. I used to fear death; but life has been so bitter, I am glad to go, yes, quite glad.'

Then she said many sweet words to me of all I had done for her, and she bid me give her love to the Chanter, and say she hoped he would forgive her.

My husband was with her most of that last day, but he saw how deeply tried and worn I was, and took me home and bid me rest, and he would return quickly.

It was near midnight when I heard his welcome step, and ran out to greet him. He folded me to his breast, saying,—

'She's at rest, dear heart, at rest, and peace is written on her face, whence all the scars are wiped out by the hand of Death. She looks almost young again.'

We laid Adelicia in her grave in our little churchyard on All Hallow's Day. Edmund stood at the head of the grave, while the Chanter Dr Crespion, .

stood at the foot. My husband read our beautiful
service, and, as ever, it brought hope and consolation
with it.

So bright and gay, I remembered Adelicia, full of
life, and pleased with admiration, which she courted
and often received.

As a little craft setting out over a summer sea, with
the sails all set to meet the gentle breeze, but with no
pilot on board, no guide to warn of rocks and quicksands; none to take the helm and bear it safe to
port; battered and forlorn after storms, yet making
the port at last, with tattered sails and broken masts,
but a wreck of its former self—such was Adelicia,
and of her, even when long years have passed, I can
only think with sadness and yet thanksgiving that
by God's mercy she reached the haven where she
would be.

My husband and Mr Crespion had much grave talk,
the evening of Adelicia's funeral, on the subject of
the Non-Jurors.

'It is certain,' Mr Crespion said, 'that the Archbishop will hold out, and that the Bishops will follow
his example. The Bishop of Bath and Wells pos-
sesses the greatest influence, and though he has
faltered a little in his resolution, yet there seems but
little doubt he will be deprived. The King is obstinate, though it is said the Queen is unwilling to

enforce the oaths on those who are unwilling to take them. What are your views?' Mr Crespion asked of my husband. 'Have you arrived at any decision?'

'Yes. And by God's help I will not draw back.'

'What! give up this fair home, and make yonder bride of yours a wanderer? Nay, nay, think better of it, dear sir; think better of it.' Then turning to me, Mr Crespion said, 'Sure you will grieve, madam, to leave this pleasant rectory. After all, one king is the same as another. You take the oaths to the holder of the office, not to the man who holds it.'

'Ah, sir,' my husband said, 'that is mere sophistry. An oath is an oath, and we must not forswear ourselves.'

'Well, well, I will not grumble at you when the Primate of all England sets the pattern. They say Tillotson is to jump into Lambeth, and he will be nothing loth; and the Bishopric of Bath and Wells is a pretty piece of preferment. Such a palace! It's like an old baronial castle, with keep and bastions, and gardens like those of Eden. I have been the Bishop's guest there, and I think it's the loveliest spot on earth.'

'And how fares it with my dear friends at Westminster, sir?' I asked, willing to change the subject of discourse.

'They are well and hearty,' was the reply. 'The boy Edward is lusty and strong, and Mistress Purcell's health is mightily improved since the boy's birth. Purcell, it may be, is taking too much extra work on himself—too much theatre work—but he is a born musician, and the Chapter are ready to overlook faults to retain him. He is sweet-tempered and obliging, thus he makes many friends. Do you hear aught of your sister, Mrs Mountfort?' Mr Crespion asked of Leonard.

'Susanna is, in fact, my cousin,' was the reply, 'but she will always have it she is my sister. She is on the stage again with her husband, who has returned to it, as you know, since the Chancellor's fall. To think of that proud, arrogant fellow asking for protection from the mob in the Tower! He was near torn to pieces by the fury of those who cannot forget the Bloody Assize.'

'It ever seems to me,' Mr Crespion said, 'a vastly strange friendship that existed between William Mountfort and Jeffreys, though it is not uncommon to see opposites in character coming together.'

Mr Crespion returned to Westminster the next day, not without expressing his obligations to me and Leonard for what we had been able to do for his poor niece. He would fain ask to reimburse us for expenses, but this we assured him could not be. Edmund Pelham had done all, and more than was needful.

'He is a rising man at the Bar, and accounted an acute lawyer, I hear,' Mr Crespion said. 'But with all due respect to you, Master Perceval, I hear he is ever in coffee-houses and places where the less respectable of the theatre folk resort. No doubt your sister and her husband are not to be reckoned amongst them, and for all scandal-mongers have to say, I believe Mistress Bracegirdle is a pure, good woman.'

'Oh, sir,' I exclaimed, 'I can vouch for it!' and then the hot colour rose to my face. I feared Leonard might think me over bold thus to speak to the Chanter.

'Yes, yes, I believe you are right;' and seeing my blushes, Mr Crespion said, 'Mistress Bracegirdle has a good friend in you, Mistress Perceval, and so have the inhabitants of Dean's Yard. The old lady, Purcell's mother, has taken up her abode there now, and there are little vexations and contrari-nesses which mothers-in-law are clever in creating.' Mr Crespion laughed, saying, 'You do not possess that relative, Master Perceval, and I dare to say you don't deplore the want of one.'

CHAPTER X

I SAID at the outset that my own life had not been marked by any very startling events, save as I was brought into contact with others whose names are known, and, as in the case of my dear master, Mr Purcell, held deservedly in remembrance.

I will pass over without many details the next two, or even three, years. They were peaceful and happy, ah! happier than any that had gone before.

Leonard was deprived of his cure, and a fat, well-conditioned man, who was easy going and good natured, took up his quarters at Burton Rectory.

It was by God's good providence that I had a home at Ivy Farm, and we removed thither in the springtime of 1690.

The little, neglected church of the parish of Hertsbury, to which parish Ivy Farm belonged, was left to take care of itself by a non-resident vicar. He had but seldom ministered there, paying a dull, careless substitute to do so at intervals. The Vicar was a rich man, and held two other livings in different parts of the county, so that, little by little, the inhabitants, like myself in old days, had preferred to cross the fields to Burton for the ministrations of my husband in that church.

I will not pretend that it was no trial for me to leave our home, and it was a greater trial for Leonard. Such goods and chattels as we needed we took away with us, and my desire was to make all things as easy as possible for Leonard. His books were his most precious possession, and I turned out the old storeroom and put the volumes in order on the shelves which my stepmother had always filled with various condiments, spices, preserves of apples, and the like.

My husband took a journey to seek the opinion of the good Bishop Ken as to the manner in which he should hold the service of the church, for although a Non-Juror, and for this cause unable to receive any of the emoluments as a clergyman, he was an ordained priest and must say the office morning and evening, according to his ordination vow.

During Leonard's absence I set myself to consider whether one of the barns could be set apart as a sort of oratory or private chapel, and with Mrs

Turner's assistance, and the good Joyce's, who followed us from Burton, declaring she would have
no wage but the honour of serving us, the barn
was not only cleared, but the bare walls hung
with some old tapestry we discovered in a chest.
I got an oak table, and setting it at the eastern end,
I covered it with a cloth, on which I wrought a
border with silks left of a store Mrs Purcell had
given me when I was embroidering a chrisom robe
for the baby Edward.

There was only a square opening, scarce to be
called a window, in the barn, but my good serving-
man fitted it with a shutter to keep out rain and
storm, and I looked forward to get it glazed when
the cost was determined.

It was what the poet Milton called a dim, religious light in our little sanctuary, but it was a
happy day for me when I saw my husband's glad
surprise on his return, and calling the household
together the next morning he read the service of
the Church, and then prayed for the blessing of
God on the humble place where we desired to
worship Him.

I found it was a sore trouble to Leonard to learn
how many of the Non-Jurors were turned out of
house and home, and often with many children,
and no means of subsistence.

'We are rich in this world's goods, dear heart,' he said, 'when we compare our lot with that of many. I have taken note of some of the most needy cases, and we must deny ourselves all needless luxury to assist our poorer brethren. You are ready to agree to this?'

How could I do other than agree? How could I do other than enter heart and soul into the plans formed by my husband for the relief of his necessitous brethren?

As I look back on those years, it may be there were little trials and vexations, but they have left no trace behind them. The great flood of an all-pervading love has effaced them from memory. I seem only to think of myself in those days as the happy wife of a noble-hearted man, who would never bate one inch of the ground on which he had taken his stand for conscience sake.

If he had needed any confirmation in the line of conduct he had chosen, he would have had it in the almost cheerful bravery of the Bishop of Bath and Wells. What it was to him to leave his beloved cathedral city—scarce more than a cathedral village; to quit the beauteous palace, where he entertained the poor at his hospitable board; to say farewell to the fair grounds, with their close-shaven lawns and terrace, where at eventide, like one of old, he meditated and uttered words of praise in the hymn which is dear to every Christian heart—who can tell?

'Sure, with such an example before me,' my husband said, 'I can scarce think of my own deprivation. I have a home, with a wife who loves me; nay, I am too much favoured, and I must do my part, to show my thankfulness to God, who has been so gracious to me.'

In the spring of the next year, what I had known must come happened, and it was with many misgivings I went to the hostel to meet the stage which brought back Madge. How often have I taken note of the strange difference presented between anticipation and reality.

Do we not often look forward to some future and wished-for good, and when it comes, it has far less of delight in it than we had fancied. And often something we dread and think of as a cloud likely to darken the brightness of our sky turns out to be a blessing. It was so in this case.

Madge, still filled with life and spirit, still free spoken, still of an independent nature, came to take up her abode with us, to be as a sunbeam, not as a cloud, in our home. She was now a tall maiden of sixteen, and she had made such good use of her schooling that for the last year she had been kept free of charge for her services in teaching other scholars.

She surprised me by the rapture of her greeting, and she told me she wanted to help me and to live with me always.

' I will do all you tell me. I will try to make amends.'

' For what?' I asked.

' Don't you know that I know how ill you were used by poor mother—by us all?'

I bid her say naught that was harsh of the dead.

' Well,' she said, ' I will speak only of the living —of myself. When I saw you devote your whole time and strength to my sick mother, whom you had small cause to love, I said naught then, but it went to my heart, and I vowed I would love you always, and serve you to my last breath. There, now, do you understand?'

There are, sure, moments like these in our lives when the reward granted us for some poor service rendered seems too much. It was so with me then. I fell weeping on Madge's neck, and the compact of our love was sealed, never to be broken.

1691. The February of this year was marked by the birth of my dear daughter Frances, named as a sign of my friendship with her godmother, Mrs Purcell of Westminster, for absence did not weaken my love for my dear master and his wife, and it was a great joy to me when Mrs Purcell consented to be my child's sponsor, and agreed to bring her babes to Ivy Farm.

We had room and to spare in our rambling old house for them, and a warm welcome to give them.

It was now that I found Madge so helpful. She had a happy way of entertaining little ones, and Frances Purcell and little Edward were taken daily by her into the fields, returning with daisy chains and cowslip balls, with the rosy hue of health on their faces.

My own babe was scarce ever out of my sight, either in my arms or in the cradle by my chair. She was a marvellous quiet infant, and her cries were few. Thus Mrs Purcell and I had ample time for talk undisturbed. I had much to hear and much to tell.

'My husband,' Mrs Purcell said, one morning, when we were together in our sunny parlour, 'deplored Master Perceval's decision, but I shall tell him you need no pity. You have a pleasant home and you look the picture of contentment. You have better health than I was ever blessed with,' and

Mrs Purcell sighed. 'You have a husband always near you and tending you, while mine is now so full of commissions and continuous work I see but little of him.'

'Surely,' I said, 'you are more than ever proud of him?'

'Yes, proud! How can I help it? But, all the same, I would fain see more of him; and I sometimes fear he is sapping away his strength by too late hours, and by being at the beck and call of all who choose to use his wonderful gifts. Master Dryden's notice and friendship pleases him mightily. He is a great man, no doubt, but he serves his own ends by making much ado over my husband. In the Preface to "King Arthur," Master Dryden says he was guided entirely by my husband in preparing it for the stage.'

As Mrs Purcell talked to me of all the events in the world of London I felt myself ignorant. My whole thoughts of late had been centred on the deprived clergy, and of doing my part in helping Leonard to send what we could spare for the sustenance of many who were well nigh starving.

Music was as ever my delight, and I played on the harpsichord and tuned the viol for singing verses of the Psalms in our little chapel, but as Mrs Purcell

spoke of the play 'King Arthur,' amongst other
things, I had to confess I had never heard of it.

Mrs Purcell laughed, saying,—

'You are happy if ignorant; but Henry bid me
instruct you in his late successes, and especially in
this friendship with Master Dryden. I laugh in my
sleeve when I hear that Master Dryden is often
in fear of arrest for debt, and finds it mighty con-
venient to go to Henry's apartment in the Clock
Tower at St James's Palace, where he is safe and
enjoys the air and scene.'

Again I was surprised. I had not heard of my
dear master, by virtue of his Court appointment,
having this apartment at St James's Palace, and
this and much more was news to me.

'No wonder Master Dryden writes, in his Dedi-
cation to " King Arthur,"' Mrs Purcell said, '"that
nothing in the play was better than the music, which
has arrived at a greater perfection than formerly,
especially passing through the artful hands of
Master Purcell, who has composed it with so
great a genius."'

'This is high praise,' I said, 'and must be sweet
to you.'

'Ay, sweet, but bitter with it,' she replied. 'What
if my husband's health breaks down—all Master
Dryden's soft words won't build it up. He has

given up the post of copyist to the Abbey, and quite right he is to do so. He missed your help at first, Betty, but he has employed several youths to aid him now. As for me, I find the children's needs as much as I can get through. You are now in the happiest time of a mother's life, with your first child content and healthy. How different was my lot—giving birth to my first-born only to see him die! I mourn my dead babes still!'

'But you have the joy of two happy, healthful children. See them now coming through the pleasance bedecked with flowers, and little Edward singing as he comes.'

'Yes,' Mrs Purcell said, 'he sings in tune and hums airs his father plays him in a wonderful fashion. He has got music in him, and Henry is set on bringing him on to follow in his steps.'

Madge now came in with the children, making such a hullabaloo that my baby started and whimpered. Edward flung himself in his mother's arms, and Frances hung a daisy chain round her neck. A pretty scene, I thought, though Mrs Purcell had scarce enough control over her children.

'I will have more,' I thought, in that proud self-satisfaction which is often seen in those who are as yet ignorant of the toils, as well as the pleasures' of motherhood.

In good sooth my Frances has borne out the character accorded her in her infant days, of being the best-tempered and most-easy-to-manage child that ever blessed a home with her presence.

Madge whispered sometimes in my ear that little Fan and Edward were over-fed, and had too much of their own way, though not with such evil results as in her case and Tom's.

'What wretches we were to you; and yet, when you were gone to Westminster, I remember sitting on the doorstep and crying till Tom came and pommelled me, and said I was a fool for my pains. Poor Tom! I was not a kind sister to him, and when he got that bad throat I ran away, poor craven that I was.'

Leonard did not fail to gain what news he could from Mrs Purcell of Susanna, for whom he had a true affection. though her marriage with William Mountfort, binding her in still closer connection with the stage and the actors, was contrary to his wishes. My husband's father was a quiet country yeoman, who had brought him up with a view to college and taking holy orders. His niece Susanna, having lost her mother when a little child, had been taken care of by Leonard's good parents, with whom she lived till both passed away—regarded more as their daughter than their

niece. Hence the great affection which had sub-
sisted between my husband and his cousin—sister,
he would often call her—and he had been much
distressed when Susanna returned to her father,
and was quickly drawn into love of the stage and
the actors and actresses.

Mrs Purcell had but little to tell me about William
Mountfort, but she said there was much talk about
Mrs Bracegirdle and her numerous admirers—none
more favoured than another—but plots had been
discovered more than once for her abduction by
lawless men, who thought only of their own
pleasure and gratification. Before Mrs Purcell left
us, she was urgent for me and the babe to travel
to Westminster and stay in Dean's Yard with her.

'You that were such a constant worshipper in
the Abbey, and a devotee of music, you must long
to be there again and hear Henry bring forth the
beauty of the organ, as no one else does. I declare,'
Mrs Purcell said, 'you shall come; this buried life,
far from every one, will get a weariness after a
time.'

'Weariness!' I said. 'How can that be, with
Leonard and my babe, the poor to succour, the
affairs of the farm to be attended to, how can I
be weary? Yes, I love Westminster, but my duty
and my highest pleasure lie here.'

P

Mrs Purcell laughed, saying, I had always been a riddle to her, and yet, she added, 'a riddle I love to find out, and I find out this much, that you are the dearest little friend I have in this world. Henry often says when he is in trouble with a chorister, or his deputy organist, or when he is hunting high and low for a sheet of music, "If Betty were here, she would soon set things right."'

This was all pleasant hearing for me, yet I was more than content to have left Westminster, the music—yes, even the music and the Abbey services—for had I not a home brightened by the sunshine of love?

The condition of the clergy who would not take the oaths became more painful as the winter drew on.

1692. In the February of the year 1692 a very extraordinary snow, for depth and continuance, made the state of the poor unhoused clergy very sad. Often, with their wives and children, they came near perishing for want of food and shelter.

The little church of Hertsbury was entirely deserted, and through all the winter months no curate came near it.

Thus Leonard felt free to invite the villagers to come to our little chapel. We had the win-

CHOIR OF WESTMINSTER ABBEY.

dow glazed now, and it was kept fairly warm
by a wood fire which we kindled on an open
hearth. Leonard having cleverly opened out a
rude sort of chimney at the farther end. Without some heat in this bitter winter we could not
have worshipped there, or asked others to do so.
It was often hard for me to think of the fair
church at Burton, not two miles away, with its
easy-tempered Rector having a service as it
suited him, and the people for whom my husband
had laboured, and done his utmost to bring into
the true and real communion with the Church—
taking good Mr George Herbert for his model—
drifting off to a conventicle, where a Puritan
teacher denounced all Church doctrine as popery,
and frightening his hearers with the terrors of hell
unless they chose to come out from her and be,
as he said, separate!

By good Joyce's assistance and Madge's help
we managed to keep broth ready for the poor,
when needed. We also baked many more
loaves than our household needed, and dispensed
these with what milk we could spare. What with
charity at home, and the money sent abroad to
our distressed fellow Non-Jurors, we were bound to
spend as little as might be on ourselves.

Leonard's cassock was much worn, and having

given his thick cloak to a poor clergyman who had begged a night's shelter, and evidently had a terrible rheum, I was sorely troubled how to replace it.

But Madge, ever quick-witted, bought, out of her own purse, a roll of black homespun from a pedlar who came to the door with his wares, and she set to work with scissors and needle, and with her clever fingers fashioned a wonderfully good cloak out of it. Enough was left to make me a cape, which she lined with some sarcenet found in a chest, then, with some skins bought of a mole-catcher, she contrived a warm wrap for my little Frances, the mole skins being so soft and silky and yet light for my baby's wear.

So we got through the winter, and many happy hours we spent by the light of a lamp hanging from the rafters in the kitchen—for we would not afford two fires—sometimes reading, sometimes singing to my viol; and when alone together, Madge, after a day's work, having gone to rest, Leonard and I would hold sweet converse together, our babe sleeping in the cradle at my feet, and scarce ever disturbing us by a cry.

Leonard also wrote and studied a great deal, always taking pains to make his sermons such as would suit his hearers—just as much pains

did he take as if he were to preach them before
the King and Queen, instead of our own labourers
on the farm and a few villagers.

One afternoon we were surprised by the appearance of Mr Blankly, the possessor of our Burton
living.

'So,' he said, 'I find you are Lord and Lady
Bountiful of the countryside. Well, well, I see
no objection, though some may say you use bribes
to get the folks to your meeting-house. You may
leave my parishioners alone, an it please you,
Master Perceval.'

Leonard was much disturbed by this view Mr
Blankly took of what we did.

'Indeed, sir,' he said, 'my old parishioners—'

'Your old parishioners,' Mr Blankly interrupted.
'They are mine now, and more fool you that it
is so.'

'Your parishioners, sir, know my mind concerning
them, namely, that I desire them to be faithful to
the church at Burton, and to be obedient to your
wishes, attend services regularly, and obey the
injunctions of the Church as to Holy Communion.'

'Well, well, I have no wish to quarrel, Master
Perceval; both you and madam seem to have stolen
the hearts of some of my people, and I suppose
I must put up with the theft, eh? But this barn

of yours is but a conventicle, and you may have some Puritan fellow bawling in it, for all you know. There's naught to prevent it.'

Leonard maintained an outward composure, but I saw by the working of his lower lip that he was greatly troubled.

'Yes, sir,' he said, 'there is something to prevent it—even my will. I would ask you to believe that those who attend the services in what you are pleased to call my barn are my own labourers chiefly, with their wives and children, and a handful of poor folk who belong to this church, the deserted church of Hertsbury, where no minister now takes any duty, and it is in fact fast going to rack and ruin.'

'That matter should be sifted,' Mr Blankly said. 'His reverence, who owns the cure, is not one of your sort, Master Perceval. He is too far sighted and sharp witted to be a Non-Juror—like me you'll say— But I'll look into it, and have him brought to task.'

I now offered Mr Blankly a cup of hot spiced ale, and some cake made by Madge. This appeared to please him; he called for a second cup, and said the ale would keep out the cold, and, he added with a smile, 'keep in the temper.'

Finally, he chucked me more familiarly than I liked under the chin, and made as if he would kiss me. But I averted this and was glad to see the last of him.

'A careless, self-seeking man,' I said. 'How can he take solemn vows upon him?'

'There are many such, Betty,' my husband said. 'They are men who look to the Church for a living, as another may look to the law, or another to trade.'

'It angers me to think,' I said, 'that you are deprived for a man like Master Blankly. It is a crying shame; it is wicked and unrighteous.'

'Gently, Betty, gently,' Leonard said. 'You must not forget that I have voluntarily given up Burton, and my successor is not to blame, being appointed by the State to succeed me.'

'I cannot help it,' I said; 'nay, I cannot help it. Master Blankly is a usurper of your rights, just as the King is a usurper of King James's.'

'Nay, sweet heart,' my husband said, 'there are two sides to all questions. No true-hearted son of the Church could desire to see the kingdom drifting back to the power of the Pope, with all the errors of doctrine and practice from which our forefathers were delivered when the yoke of Rome was shaken off. Doubtless the new rule is a blessing, though maybe in disguise.'

Soon after this Leonard began seriously to question whether he did well to remain in the near neighbourhood of the cure of which he had been deprived. Troubles arose through the emptying of the church at Burton and the filling to overflowing of our chapel.

In the autumn of this year, Leonard, after much anxious thought and prayer, decided to seek council once more of Bishop Ken as to our future. On his journey thither he caught a severe chill, and I had a messenger sent from Westminster by Mr Purcell with the dire news that my husband was under their roof in a dangerous condition, and that I must at once set forth to join him.

And now what a support I had in Madge. She helped me to put all things in order, and promised to manage the farm, and to see the serving-men did their duty.

Madge's masterful spirit and resolution were now to be of good service to me. With my babe in her arms she set out with me to the hostel whence the stage started. Old Giles, still strong and hearty, followed with the heavy baggage on a barrow, and Joyce, with a light basket filled with my baby's clothes and pap-boat.

My heart was heavy within me. It was bitter to me to say farewell to our home, to the chapel where we had so often knelt to pray, to my people and the villagers, who came out in that chill, dim October morning to wish me God-speed and to hope that I should find his reverence in better health than I feared. Madge kept up my spirits by her own bright anticipations.

'You will find him well-nigh recovered, depend on it, and you will soon be here again. Now, Joyce,' Madge said sharply, as she saw Joyce's falling tears, 'what are you making an ado for? A poor way that to cheer the mistress. Look at little Frances, how she is springing in my arms, I can scarce hold her, and laughing as she says, "Daddy! daddy! I'm going to daddy!"'

My Frances was ever a forward child, and now, at a year and eight months old, she could prattle and try to be understood.

I could not take Joyce with me, so I set forth on my long journey alone. Joyce was of great importance in the house. I could not leave Madge without her help.

I recalled my start into the unknown world beyond, when a child of scarce sixteen, and the feeling of desolation and banishment which oppressed me then. Now I had my child and I

was on my way to see my husband. It was true
I knew not how it fared with him, but, at least, I
should see him and tend him, and bring him back
at last sound and well.

The little group at the stage door waving good-
byes, my little Frances blowing kisses to them, I
can see before me now. Soon the parting was over ;
the stage rumbled off. I craned my neck out of
the unshuttered window for a last look, and I saw
Madge, who had smiled and laughed to the last
moment as she stood by the door, cover her face
with her hands, weeping bitterly.

'How she loves me !' I thought. 'God be thanked
for her, and the staff and stay she has been to me.'

The journey was long—we made but slow way, and
only those who have had to travel with a sore heart,
scarce knowing what news is waiting at the journey's
end, can tell how the dull thud of the horse's
hoofs seemed to beat into my brain, how every
jolt and every hindrance in the way seemed to be
unbearable.

Twilight faded, darkness came on, the October
day had closed in, and still on, on, and, as it
were, no nearer the end.

My child slept peacefully, while I sat with wide-
open eyes, gazing out into the gloom. Would
the journey never end?

So slow had been the progress that those thirty miles were like three hundred to my anxious heart, which grew more anxious and less hopeful every hour that passed.

'I cannot bear it much longer,' I said, as we came to a halt. A lanthorn gleamed, there were voices of men as they handed down some heavy luggage from the roof.

'Where are we?' I cried, putting my head out of the window. 'Pray tell me, is it much further to London? Oh! I pray you, tell me!'

'Six odd miles,' was the reply. 'You are in a mighty hurry, young woman.'

I drew back and, clasping my child closer to my breast, sat upright. Again the dull beat of the horses' hoofs and the jolting and rumbling of the clumsy wheels.

'I ought to pray for patience,' I said, reasoning with myself. 'Why can't I pray? Leonard would pray,' and with his name, uttered in my distress, a flood of tears poured forth, and I think my desire to pray was accepted and heard, for the frightful tension of suspense loosened, and I said, 'God's will be done.'

I was met at the hostel this time by my dear master himself. Ah, how the sound of his voice thrilled me!

He did not wait for a question, but took the child from my arms, saying,—

'Welcome, Mistress Perceval; your husband fares better than we could have hoped, and longs for your presence.'

With thoughtful kindness, Mr Purcell had a chair hired, and he placed me in it with the child, saying,—

'The baggage shall follow by a carrier. I know you are anxious to be at Westminster.'

As I have said, deep emotion ever made me dumb. I could find no words wherewith to thank my dear master. Just as the men lifted the poles, and we were swinging out of the hostel yard, I thought how ungracious I must seem. I cried out then,—

'Hold! hold! for one instant.'

The chair was set down, and Mr Purcell's head was at the window.

'What ails you, Betty?'

'Nothing, only I never thanked you for your goodness.'

'Is that all? You will have time to do that later. I am going by command to Whitehall to play before the Queen, but these chairmen will take you safe to Dean's Yard, and my wife is looking out for you. My mother is there also, so good-even to you.'

To wait on the Queen by command! Mr Purcell

must be in favour at Court! Yes, I was soon to learn that he was now courted by the noble and great, and that his fame had spread far and wide.

In another half-hour I was folded to Mrs Purcell's heart.

'What is it?' I asked. 'What ails my husband?'

'He has had a bleeding from the chest, but the danger is past; only you must be wary—he is not to speak.'

I was about to take my child to the chamber where Leonard lay, when old Mrs Purcell shook her head.

'No, no, give her to me.'

I did my utmost to be calm, but my knees seemed to refuse to bear me up the stairs.

Leonard received me with a smile, and as I bent over him, he whispered,—

'God has decided for me. I shall never return to Hertsbury.'

'Hush! dear heart, you must not speak.'

He smiled again, and closed his eyes, holding my hand in a firm grasp, and I thanked God I was with him.

BOOK VI

1692-1694

'In quietness and in confidence shall be your strength.
—ISAIAH xxx. 15.

CHAPTER XI

IT soon became apparent that my husband, though delivered from the near approach of death, was in a condition for which rest and quiet, ay, and silence, were the only remedies.

To return to Ivy Farm was impossible, and to intrude on the household of Mr Purcell for any prolonged time appeared to us both an encroachment on his friendship and goodness, and that of Mrs Purcell. Their circumstances had changed since I first entered their house.

Mr Purcell was now much in request in the circles of the nobility, giving lessons on harpsichord and organ, and often commanded to appear at Whitehall to perform before the Queen.

Mr Purcell's intimacy with Mr Dryden also conspired to bring him to the notice of all poets or rhymesters, who hung about him with requests

Q

that he would write music to some song or ballad which was mostly beneath his notice as a composer.

Susanna Mountfort came often to get tidings of Leonard's state.

She was truly attached to him, but her conversation, lively as it was, had reference to things in which he had no interest, and ofttimes he was weary of her well-intended anecdotes.

But she was of use to me in the dilemma I found myself as to what our future was to be. She told me of part of a house in Duke Street, where Mrs Arabella Hunt, a singer and performer on the lute, had lived, and was now moving to better quarters, and would fain let out the rooms in it on hire.

It would be an easy removal to the house, and I went to inspect it, with the view of taking it as soon as Leonard could be removed thither.

I found Mrs Hunt very ready to accommodate me, and in spite of Mrs Purcell's remonstrances I decided to accept Mrs Hunt's offer.

The removal was effected with greater ease than I had feared, and Mrs Hunt was out of the house about the middle of November; and having good supplies from our farm, sent by carrier by Madge, with money also from the proceeds of the harvest, we were at ease, and thankful to be in our own home again.

A good serving-maid was part of the bargain, and I was thus set free to attend continually to the wants of him who was dearest to me in the world.

Little Frances throve apace, and many an hour's anxiety was whiled away by her innocent prattle and her sunny temper. I know all mothers, looking back over the past years, are prone to think no babes equal to what their own were, yet I do affirm, from first to last, my Frances was as the angel of my life and the darling of her sick father's heart.

Leonard was not idle. As soon as he could wield a pen he began to write short discourses and explanations of the service book of the Church, which, as he said, might be useful now his voice could no longer be heard. I made fair copies of these, and sent them, one or two at a time, to Madge, instructing her to read them to the people when they came to hear the lessons and psalms read by her twice a day in our little chapel.

The people loved thus to listen to their dear master's words, and, though absent in body, he was present with them in spirit.

Madge, who wrote a wondrous clear hand, was faithful to me and to my interests, and she kept a diary, which she sent in parts weekly by the stage, with the parcels of home produce, cakes, manchets of fine bread, conserves of apples just ready, and other dainties which might tempt Leonard's appetite.

I found my way, as often as I could leave my husband, to the much-loved Abbey, and on Sunday to the Chapel Royal, where Mr Purcell had brought the choir well-nigh to a state of perfection. The Reverend Mr Gostling, my early friend, was still a chorister there, and his bass voice had lost nothing of its depth and richness.

He came to visit me soon after we were settled in Duke Street, and gave us news of the outer world, of which we knew as little as when we were at Hertsbury.

I must record one of his visits here, because Mr Gostling gave us the first note of warning as to the increased spite and malevolence displayed by certain admirers of Mrs Bracegirdle, which were noticed in many quarters, 'Your good cousin, Mistress Mountfort, sir,' he said, addressing my husband, 'may have told you.'

Leonard shook his head.

'Nay,' he said, 'we have heard nothing of this; but we live not in the world, though so near it.'

'Well, well, let it pass! I may be a croaking

raven, but I know full well jealousy is cruel as the grave. Here is a young poetaster appeared of late, who has fallen, like many another, at Mistress Bracegirdle's feet. His name is Congreve, and there is an amazing hot alliance between him and Master Dryden. He is everywhere about the town—in the Park and the playhouse and the coffee-house. They say that from the first moment he saw Mistress Bracegirdle in one of her best parts, he swore he would write a play worthy of her, and bring her fame which should throw all that has preceded it into the shade. So,' said Mr Gostling, 'here is another added to Mistress Bracegirdle's lovers, and another cause of danger added to some who win her favour and the hatred of those who fail to do so. I believe Anne Bracegirdle to be a pure, good woman,' Mr Gostling said; 'but who is safe from slanderous tongues when exposed, as she is, to the publicity of the theatre?'

I had never forgotten Mrs Bracegirdle and my adoration of her, so that all I could hear of her was eagerly listened to.

Mr Gostling told us on another occasion that Queen Mary had been much taken by the melody of an old ballad, 'Cold and raw,' which all the young ruffians sang through the streets.

'For my part,' Mr Gostling said, 'though I have sung the bass part in it many a time and oft I never thought it would be honoured as it has been by a queen's notice. One afternoon the Queen, minded to be diverted by music—and, poor soul! I think she needs diversion from troubled thoughts—sent off for me and Henry Purcell and Mistress Arabella Hunt, in whose room we are now sitting, to sing and play to her. My bass and Mistress Hunt's fine treble and pretty lute playing, with Henry Purcell on the harpsichord, made a charming "concord of sweet sounds." Henry Purcell's songs are ever full of music, and the Queen was pleased, we hoped. At last the Queen suddenly said to Mistress Hunt,—

'"That is all fine grave music; sing me the old Scots ballad beginning 'Cold and raw.'"

'Mistress Hunt tuned her lute and sang it twice; the Queen, clapping her hands and laughing, beat her small feet to the time.

'I saw a cloud gathering on Henry Purcell's face as he sat by the harpsichord with his fingers idle before him. But his sweet temper soon conquered the chagrin he felt.

'As we left the presence of the Queen together, he said,—

'"By my faith, if the Queen is so taken by a

vulgar little ballad, and finds it better than our music, she shall have it."

'So, in the birthday song of this year, in the lovely air Purcell has composed to the words, "May her bright example," the bass is the very tune of "Cold and raw," note for note the same, showing not only Purcell's good nature but his genius, for who but he could have wedded the matchless air of his own beautiful composition to the common tune of the old ballad?

'He seems to me a greater marvel every day,' Mr Gostling said, 'but I do not like his looks at times. His eyes are too bright—they burn with the hidden fire, and there is a restlessness in him—to be ever reaching forward to attain more than he has yet attained.'

Mr Gostling's visits always cheered and entertained my husband. He had the great gift of never seeming hurried.

Sick folk always chafe against those who come to see them, and say they have but a few minutes to spare and must haste away. Mrs Purcell and Susanna had something of this haste about them.

'No sooner here than gone again,' Leonard said one day, with a sigh, when Susanna had come in, filled with the success of a play she had taken part in with Mrs Bracegirdle and

Mrs Barry; 'but I want no other companions than my little Frances and her mother.'

It was a December day when a message was brought up to Leonard's chamber that a gentlewoman was waiting to see me in the parlour below.

'On particular business,' our serving-maid said.

For one instant it flashed over me that it might be Madge, bearing bad news from Ivy Farm, and I went down in a state of wonder and alarm.

A figure in a long cloak and hood drawn close over her face advanced towards me.

'This is Mistress Perceval.' A voice clear as a bell — like music — repeated, 'This is Mistress Perceval.'

'Yes,' I cried. 'Yes, and you are Mistress Bracegirdle. No one has a voice like yours.'

'Ah! is it so?' she said, throwing back her hood, and displaying her beautiful face, not wreathed in smiles now, but with an anxious, troubled look in her lovely eyes. 'I am come to beg you to do me a service.'

'Oh! madam, there is nothing I would not do to serve you,' I replied.

Mrs Bracegirdle sank down on the nearest chair, and said,—

'Dear child! I have not forgot you. You are married to Susanna Mountfort's brother.'

'Her brother by affection, madam, but in truth her cousin.'

'Ah! I had heard as much. Now hearken! for time presses. There is a plot hatched, or hatching, which means ruin to me. That brave and true man, William Mountfort, has a suspicion of it. He has set himself to find out how it is to be accomplished, determined to frustrate their evil designs. I want you, Mistress Perceval, or Betty—little Bet—I must still call you, to give William Mountfort's wife warning that these wicked men would fain get rid of him. By no means suffer him to go out of his house this night on any pretext whatsoever. He is looked on as my guardian, and thus he is their enemy who would fain carry me off. Not,' she said, speaking with all the fire which she could put into her words—'not that they will gain their wicked ends. I would run a knife through the villain first, ere he got possession of me, ere he touched a hair of my head. If I went to Susanna Mountfort, it would be found out, it would rouse suspicion; but if you go ostensibly to inform her of your husband's state, or to take her a letter from him, it will seem but a natural thing. Will you do this?'

'When, madam?'

'Before nightfall—now.'

'Yes, madam,' I said; 'I will do your bidding, though first I must gain my husband's leave.'

'No, you must not divulge your errand, even to him.'

'I cannot hide aught from my husband,' I said. 'He will keep the secret well; there is no one to whom he can confide it; it is safe. He never leaves his sick chamber; except for myself and baby daughter, but few enter it.'

'Start quickly,' Mrs Bracegirdle said; 'do not delay, I beseech you, I pray you.'

Who could resist Mrs Bracegirdle? Her pleading voice, her hands clasped in entreaty.

'I must hasten away; my chair and servants await me. I dare not delay, nor do you delay, and may God prosper your errand and reward you.' She put her arms around me, and gazing down into my face, she said, 'You look guileless as ever—a child still, and happy.'

'Nay, madam,' I said, 'I am a proud wife and mother, and I have known sorrow. My husband has been deprived of his living, and he is very sick, so that he will, the physician says, never use his voice again without danger to life.'

Mrs Bracegirdle kissed me once more, saying in a low whisper,—

'It is life or death—life or death, remember,' and then she drew her cloak round her and was gone.

I stood for a moment where she had left me, and questioned whether I should tell Leonard of the errand to Susanna Mountfort. I decided that he must know, for I left him so seldom, and my absence unexplained would cause him anxiety.

At first he was unwilling I should undertake a walk through the streets unprotected, but when I repeated Mrs Bracegirdle's words, ' It is life or death,' he gave way and bid me perform my errand before the short day closed in.

I rose up with a good courage, and found the streets in Westminster less full of people than I had feared.

I could not resist the impulse, and turned into the Abbey, where, evensong over, Mr Purcell was playing the organ.

I knelt on the hard pavement as I had knelt years before, and prayed for help, and that God would take me under His protection—a woman threading her way alone through the streets of the city.

I rose up strengthened, and set forth again, not

running, as I felt much disposed to do, for fear of attracting attention.

A group of gentlemen were standing round the door of a coffee house as I passed, and the footway was blocked.

I turned off into the road, when one of them cried,—

'Whither away?' and laid a hand on my cloak, trying with the other to lift my hood. 'A fair face, forsooth! Come, let us see more on't.'

I summoned all my courage, and, instead of struggling, I said firmly,—

'I must beg you, sir, to let me pass. I am abroad on urgent business.'

A laugh, joined in by another man, was accompanied by the words,—

'I'll warrant it is urgent, but your lover must wait. You must give us a slice of your company first, and let us drink your health in a mug of good wine.'

My courage began to fail, and my heart beat fast, but I turned on my tormentors and said,—

'Leave me to pursue my way, nor attempt to detain me, if you call yourselves honourable gentlemen.'

'Well spoken. The Bracegirdle could not surpass this. A veritable tragedy queen.'

And now, to my relief, help came. Another man came out of the coffee house to see what was happening.

It was Edmund Pelham. He thrust aside the two men and cried,—

'For shame! to molest a gentlewoman in this fashion.'

'Oh! Edmund,' I cried, 'help me!'

In another moment he had drawn my hand in his arm, and, turning upon the men, said,—

'This gentlewoman is under my protection, and I will conduct her to her destination. You might well go down on your knees and crave her pardon for your unmannerly behaviour.'

A mocking laugh was the rejoinder, and one of the men said,—

'I am well pleased that this gentlewoman is under such safe conduct. I hope she will be duly grateful to her deliverer.'

'Whither are you going, Betty?' Edmund asked.

'To Mr Mountfort's house. I have a message for his wife.'

'It is ill done of your husband to let you go through the streets unprotected. Methinks it shows but scant devotion to you.'

'Do not speak thus of my husband, Edmund. He is laid on a sick couch, whence it is doubtful whether he ever rises. I came with his leave, but the reason for doing so is what I can tell to no one.'

'Not even to me?' Edmund said. 'Not even to me?'

'No,' I replied, 'certainly not to you.'

'Well, you have come out of your way to Mountfort's house. A chance if you find either him or his wife in their house when you get there. They have a play rehearsing, which is to be a grand affair. Mistress Mountfort is acting as well as her husband, and made much of.'

It was as Edmund Pelham said. When we reached the Mountforts' house in Norfolk Street, in the Strand, we were told by a young woman, whom we found sitting in the midst of a heap of finery for the stage, which she was adapting to the character Susanna was to take, that it was likely Mrs Mountfort would return ere long.

Then I must await her return,' I said. 'I have a message for her which must be delivered by myself.'

The seamstress, for this she was, threw a log on the hearth, gathered up a handful of brocades and gold lace, and left the parlour.

Edmund still lingered, and, as I looked at him, my heart was filled with sadness on his account.

The handsome face was still handsome, but there

was but little left of the Edmund whose coming had been the looked-for pleasure of my childhood at Ivy Farm.

There were traces on his face and in his whole bearing of one who had drunk deep of the pleasures of the world. He was extravagantly dressed, his hair perfumed, his curls tied with a gold and red riband. In the midst of all my anxious thought as to my errand and how it was to be accomplished, I gave thanks that I was the wife of a man like my husband, even though he lay sick, and was, so the physician said, not like to be ever sound in health again.

Edmund talked with well-chosen words, and gave me tidings of my stepmother's sons—both in the Navy, and one distinguished for valour in the battle of the Boyne. Notice had been taken of him by Mr Pepys, and he was sure to be promoted.

Edmund was obliged, he said, to meet a man who had entrusted him to defend a suit in Chancery, and therefore, when the clock struck six, he left me, saying he would return and conduct me to Dean's Yard, unless William Mountfort did it.

An hour's solitude and watching followed. A servant brought in fresh firewood, and said Mrs Mountfort would be at home ere long, for she had bid her prepare supper at seven o'clock.

I remembered Mrs Bracegirdle's words,—

'On no account whatsoever let William Mountfort leave his house this evening.'

Now I found he had left it, and how could I give the warning to Susanna which she desired. At last she came in, throwing off her cloak and saying she had gone over her part till she was sick in Mr Congreve's play, 'The Old Bachelor,' where Mrs Bracegirdle was to act Araminta.

'That is a good part, worthy of a fine actress; but mine is a trumpery one and I shall try to get a better. There is time. The play can't be on the boards till after Christmas now.' I think Susanna saw I looked grave, and scarcely heeded what she said. 'Is Leonard worse?' she asked. 'I think you keep him too dull and moped; he wants to be roused and amused. Master Congreve's play would make even Leonard laugh.'

'I did not come hither about Leonard,' I said. 'I bring a message from Mistress Bracegirdle that your husband was by no means to leave the house this evening.'

'How is that? What does she mean? You speak in riddles, Betty. Mistress Bracegirdle was not at the rehearsal. It was only the subordinate folk like myself who were there. Neither was William there. What can this mean?'

'I fear me, Susanna,' I said, 'it means there is danger to William's life.'

'I cannot believe it; and if it be so, what am I to do?'

'Can you find out where he is, so that a messenger could be sent to him?'

'To tell him not to leave the house when he has left it! How foolish you are, Betty!'

'Well, foolish or not, I have delivered my message, and I would beg you not to disregard it. Mistress Bracegirdle appeared greatly distressed.'

I don't know how it was that Susanna took what I said lightly. She seemed determined not to be alarmed.

At last, feeling I could do no more, I said,—

'I am anxious to go back to my husband. Edmund Pelham promised to return for me.'

'Then, wait till he appears. Dear heart, I would that I knew where Will is; but as he was not at the theatre, I am at a loss. I wish he were safe in the house.'

So did I, most earnestly.

Presently we heard voices in the street below. The parlour was on the second floor, and as the voices grew louder and louder, and a cry as of one in pain rang through the still air of the December night, Susanna opened the lattice and looked out.

R

'There is a riot,' she said. 'There is a scuffle just at our door. Come down, Betty, and let us see what it means.'

Meanwhile the hubbub in the street grew louder and louder.

I followed Susanna down the stairs and heard her cry, almost scream,—

'Who is it?—who is hurt?'

Edmund Pelham's voice answered,—

'Mr Mountfort is wounded. We have hold of one of the miscreants; the other—'

'William! Will, oh, my dear Will!' for two men were slowly bearing upstairs the nearly lifeless form of William Mountfort, the blood pouring from a wound in his side.

He was laid upon the couch, groaning terribly. His wife flung herself on her knees by his side, and was beside herself with terror and grief.

They had summoned the nearest surgeon, and, till he came, I tore off my kerchief and tried to staunch the wound.

All in vain. The life-blood ebbed fast, and the pallor of death was on Mountfort's fair and beautiful face. He recovered the power of speech, and said in a far-away voice,—

'Susanna, dear wife, hearken! I have been absent all day doing my best to frustrate the wicked

design of the man that has killed me—for I am
dying.'

'No, no, Will! You must not die!' Susanna
cried.

'Hush! dear love, and hearken. Tell *her* I have
died for her sake, and if I have saved her from
that villain, I—I am content.'

In the corner of the room, where by this time
many people were collected, a boy stood shuddering
and terror-struck. Two men held him in a firm
grip, and he seemed like one paralysed with fear.
I heard them say it was Lord Mohun, a mere lad
of scarce seventeen years old.

Presently William Mountfort turned his dying
eyes on the culprit, and said in a whisper, growing
fainter and fainter each word he spoke,—

'He did not strike the blow. It was Hill—Captain Hill. Where is he?'

'Escaped in the first moments of confusion,' Edmund Pelham said; 'but the constables are on the
track.'

'Thank God! his designs are frustrated, and he
will now fear to pester a good woman. The
bird has escaped the snare of the fowler. Give
God thanks, dear Sue.'

As far as I know, these were the last words that
fell from those pale lips.

Before long the news had spread, and William Mountfort's friends came from the theatre—Mrs Barry, with Mr Perceval, Susanna's father, and others.

The house was full of indignant questioners, vowing vengeance on William's murderer.

'The brutal cowardice of the villain to hit him from behind!' Mr Perceval said. 'That wretched boy cowering yonder must be held as guilty as if he had stabbed my poor son-in-law. He held him talking, to let Hill come up.'

I struggled hard against a feeling of faintness which came over me, but it was in vain. I had just made my way out of the parlour, when I should have fallen headlong, had not someone saved me.

It was Mrs Bracegirdle.

'So you have failed me,' she said; 'I can never forgive you. I trusted you, and you have failed to do my bidding. A noble life is lost.'

Her words roused me, and, with streaming tears, I faltered out,—

'Nay, do not reproach me, madam; I made my way hither, and waited for the return of Mistress Mountfort. When she came, I prayed her to find out where Master Mountfort was, and she could not tell me; she did not know. I did my utmost, and your reproaches wring my heart.'

'Poor child! poor child! I would not be harsh to you—but, oh! hearken!—hearken!'

For the groans of one in mortal agony fell on our ears from the parlour where the dying man lay.

I broke away. I was not wanted. I could do naught to help, and I knew Leonard would be in distress at my long absence.

Ah! what thankfulness filled my heart when a well-known voice came from the crowd at the door.

'Oh! Master Purcell,' I cried, 'take me home—take me to my husband.'

'Betty! What can have brought you to this scene of horror and confusion?'

'I cannot tell you now—only help me to get home!'

Mr Purcell asked no further questions. He put his arm round me and drew me through the crowd which blocked the street—some crying vengeance on the murderer, and threatening to tear Lord Mohun in pieces if they could get at him.

A terrible scene, indeed; and, as I write of that December night, all the dread and horror come back to me.

Mr Purcell saw a chair standing, with servants

and torches, at the further end of the street, which opened into a square.

'Here,' he said, 'take this gentlewoman to Duke Street, and you shall have your reward.'

'This chair, sir, is Mistress Bracegirdle's. We have just put her down; we are not at liberty to allow any one else to make free with it.'

'Mistress Bracegirdle shall hear from me that this gentlewoman has made use of her chair. I am well-known to her, and so is Mistress Perceval.'

Then, without more ado, he ordered the men to lift the roof of the chair, and, helping me into it, he repeated his orders and in another moment I felt myself borne away at a rapid pace.

The chair was a luxurious one furnished with satin cushions, into which, weary and overcome with all I had gone through, I sank back exhausted.

I had no money wherewith to pay the men, but I detached a small locket from a chain and said,—

'You can sell this and divide the price a goldsmith will give you, and tell your mistress, Mistress Betty Perceval sends her thanks for the service you have rendered her.'

The head lacquey demurred and would not take the locket.

'Nay, madam, we take your word for it, and if we have served a friend of our good mistress we need no pay. This has been a bad night's work,' he added, 'and it will go near to break our lady's heart.'

The door of the house was quickly opened and our good serving-maid cried,—

'Thank God you are safe, madam! The master—'

I waited to hear no more but flew up the stairs to Leonard's room. Then I paused at the door ere I lifted the latch. I feared to do him harm if I entered in too much haste. I tried to still the beating of my heart, and went softly into the chamber.

Oh, the joy of kneeling down by my husband's couch and hearing him say,—

'You have been long—very long away, sweetheart; but I committed you to God's keeping and felt secure that you would return unharmed.'

'Unharmed, yes ; but all was in vain. The warning was not in time, and William Mountfort has been foully murdered.'

'Ah! what tidings! Poor, bereft Susanna! and I lie here and can do naught to comfort her. You shall tell me all details when you have rested. See, here is our good Mattie with a cup of wine for you and a morsel of the good pasty you made this morning. My poor, brave little wife,' he said, caressing my hair and holding one of my hands firmly in his. 'You have been brave and have done your best.'

'But I have failed, Leonard—I have failed.'

'Do not dwell on this, dear heart; but when you are refreshed with the food you must surely need, you shall tell me all—not yet, not yet,' for I was rehearsing all that had happened in my mind, and a violent shuddering seized me.'

Mattie wisely held the cup to my lips, and breaking up the pasty into morsels, she fed me as she would have fed my little Fan. Then, as I grew calmer, Leonard watching me with anxious eyes, Mattie began to relate what an angel of goodness Fan had been all the long hours of my absence, and how Mrs Purcell had brought in her Master Edward, who seemed so mightily taken with my Fan he did naught but kiss her and say he would fain take her home with him, he liked her better than his little sister.

'Bring me Fan,' I said; 'let me have her in my arms. She will comfort me.'

'She is asleep in her cot; sure you would not wake her, the sweet heart.'

'Do bring her,' I repeated; 'I want to hold her in my arms.'

'Yes,' Leonard said; 'yes, Mattie, bring hither our child.'

'Ah! how sweet is the comfort a little child can give. When Mattie brought our babe, though her blue eyes were dim with slumber, her cheeks like a damask rose, she never whimpered, but smiled, saying,—

'Mother—mother is come home—kiss.'

I took her and held her close, and, her dear arms clinging to my neck, she was soon asleep again.

As I looked in her little face, pure and fair as an angel, I thought of Mrs Bracegirdle's words, 'Would that I were an innocent child playing in the cowslip fields again,' and I prayed that my sweet babe might be guarded from the wickedness of the world and kept safe from the blight of sin and of evil.

CHAPTER XII

A. D. 1693

THE murder of William Mountfort threw a gloom over the beginning of this year, and none felt the tragedy of his death more than did my husband.

He had a brother's affection for Susanna, and he deplored her widowed condition on all accounts, and hoped her father would persuade her to leave the stage, at anyrate for a time.

The miscreant, Captain Hill, made good his escape, and left the unhappy boy of scarce seventeen to be arraigned for the murder in which he had been but an accomplice.

The trial of Lord Mohun by his peers in Westminster Hall was memorable for the interest it caused, the King coming to be present at it and watching the proceedings on several days,

WESTMINSTER HALL, IN THE SEVENTEENTH CENTURY.

for the trial was drawn out to a very extra-ordinary length; and on the fifth day, though the evidence of Lord Mohun's guilt was clear, his peers acquitted him by sixty-nine votes to fourteen. Some said this was owing to pity for his youth, and that a voice was heard saying,—

'Take the boy away and whip him.'

Mr Purcell, who was present at the last day of the trial, told us this, and added,—

' If he had been whipped sooner, the better for him; he has run a long course of wickedness, young as he is, and he will now go from bad to worse. Imprison-ment would have kept him out of mischief for a few years.'

The horror of that scene in Norfolk Street had affected me very sensibly, and I was sick in body and mind, and seldom left the house.

What news we heard of the outside world was brought by Mrs Purcell, and she did her best to cheer me. It was she who brought the tidings that Susanna Mountfort was taking the part of Belinda in Mr Congreve's play of ' The Old Bachelor,' and this so soon after William's awful death.

It seemed incredible that one so lately made a widow should take a part in any play, more especi-ally one of a comic character.

' Her father permitting it removes responsibility

from me,' my husband said, 'but I must see Susanna and do my best to change her purpose.'

Susanna obeyed Leonard's summons, and came to our house in a chair, clad in the heaviest weeds of widowhood.

I had not seen her since that fearsome night, and I could scarce refrain from weeping. Susanna herself was graver than her wont, and after greeting us both and saying little Frances was an angel of beauty, she sat down by Leonard's side, saying,—

'You tell me I ought not to go on the boards so soon after Will's death. You do not know what it is to be an actress. What does it matter to Master Congreve the author, and Master Davenant the manager of the Theatre Royal if our hearts are whole or breaking? Does young Master Congreve care whether I act the witty part of Belinda with sorrow or joy so long as I do it? Not he—not he; he is adding another to the train of Anne Bracegirdle's lovers, and he will not have the play he wrote to bring her out in as Araminta spoiled by want of good supporters in the inferior parts. Think what it is to him to lose by death not only William—William, who would have taken the part of Vainlove, was at the rehearsals unrivalled—but Master Nokes and Master Leigh—both splendid in their several parts—are likewise dead! If I refuse to act, the play will suffer, and

what Master Congreve calls the quartette of beauties
will be spoiled. No, I must do it. There is no help
for it. Leonard, do not look at me thus, as if you
heard my death-warrant was signed.'

'I do look at you with sorrow,' Leonard said.
'We were children together, and your mother was
as a mother to me. Do you not recall how, when
your father took to the stage and left his home to
follow the profession, she kept you close to her
side? And when you mimicked the old people in
the village and made me laugh at your clever hits,
she would look sad and grave? Think of your
mother, dear Sue.'

'Think of her!' she exclaimed passionately. 'I
never forget her, but I am praised and applauded
by my father, and Will was so proud of me. Oh!
my poor, lost William!'

Then a flood of tears and sobs and cries, as if
her heart were breaking, made Leonard draw her
closer and soothe her as though she were his own
little Frances.

I left them together, and after half-an-hour had
passed, Susanna came out of the chamber, and,
bidding me a hasty farewell, ran quickly to the
door, where her chair awaited her.

The play of 'The Old Bachelor' was a marvellous success. The whole town was all agog

to see it, and Mr Congreve's triumph was complete.

Mr Purcell came in for much praise for the music he had composed for it, which seemed, if it were possible, to tighten the friendship between him and Mr Dryden. For Mr Dryden had conceived a very great admiration for young Mr Congreve, and it was by his means that this play of 'The Old Bachelor' was fashioned to suit the taste of the playgoers and the public at large.

It will seem that I was much bound up with theatrical folk, but I may say that, though I had been much enthralled by seeing plays acted in which Mrs Bracegirdle took part, I had an increased shrinking from the stage as a profession. I saw its perils, and, as in the case of Susanna, I saw how often the woman, even in grief, must be lost in the actress.

It is not for me to be censorious or to lay down hard rules, but often, as I looked on my own little Frances, I would pray earnestly that no allurements or persuasions, if perchance she showed a gift for acting, should lead her to take up the stage as a means of livelihood.

My health gave way at this time, and after the birth of our second child, little Elizabeth, I was reduced to a very pitiable condition of weakness.

My husband, although better, had still to be cautious as to exposure to a cold atmosphere, and the spring of this year was more like winter than spring. Snowstorms were followed by an amazing rainfall, and my babe came into a cold world indeed, and was difficult to rear in consequence. I was unable to do aught for her, and my husband, seeing how weak and helpless I was, sent for Madge to come to us, for happily Mrs Turner had taken up her abode at the farm till such time as we could return thither.

I cannot say how welcome Madge was. She was full of life and spirit, and won the praise of Mrs Purcell for her care of me.

'I thought you could not endure nursing the sick,' I said to her one day; 'and now you are the best of nurses.'

'Ah! but I have the best of sick folk to nurse; that makes it easy.'

Madge entertained us with accounts of Ivy Farm and the easy-going Rector of Burton.

'He grows fatter every day, and lives in great luxury, eating and drinking more than is good for him,' she said. 'He comes to visit me sometimes, and, although only a walk of less than two miles, he always asks for a cup of ale. No one comes

near the little church of Hertsbury, and there is a
conventicle now, hard by the mill, to which numbers
of people resort. Old Joe, the miller, sometimes preaches when there is no one besides to
do so. I could laugh to think of it. I have yet
a few faithful souls, and our own labourers, who
come to the little chapel, and I read the lessons
and Leonard's discourses, as I am bid. But I
wish you were back once more, with all my
heart.'

I began to echo that wish, and I found Leonard
was of the same mind.

'If once the summer comes,' he said, 'we will return to the farm, and I must look for some young
scholar to read the service for me, and it may be
that I shall be able to use my voice if I make but
little effort.'

I knew not how this would be, for the physician
who came to see me warned me that any undue
exertion of the voice would bring on the bleeding,
of which I had for some months lived in continual
dread lest it should happen. It was a great trial
of patience for me. I loved to be active, and free
to come and go.

Especially did I long to get into the choir of the
Abbey for refreshing and comfort when evensong
and matins were said.

But I was shut out from this, one of my chief delights, and I knew full well I was often querulous and cross-grained to Madge.

Mr and Mrs Purcell now led a very busy life. Mr Purcell was often commanded to appear at Whitehall, as the Queen loved to hear him play and Mrs Hunt sing the songs which he had set to music.

It was always a joy to me to see Mr Purcell, and he had ever, when he paid me a visit, some kind and consoling word ready. It struck me painfully on one occasion that there was a look of increasing delicacy on his face. His wide brow was, so it seemed to me, over-weighted with the constant work of the brain, from which he gave himself no rest. His beautiful eyes were unnaturally bright, and there was sometimes a short, sharp cough as he came up the stairs to my chamber.

'Let no one think, Betty,' he said, on the occasion I speak of, 'that the musician's life is free from toil. I often wonder, when the versifiers come to me, begging me to write music for their rhymes, whether they know that I bestow pains, ay, and labour too, on what seem to many, when accomplished, but trifles. It is a different matter when I write music for the Festival of St Cecilia. This is floating in my mind, and I think the *Te Deum*

S

Laudamus will be a fitting strain for those matchless words. But I have much on hand ere I can
produce this. The commemoration ode for Trinity
College is finished, and it is when my spirit is
free to give noble words a fitting expression with
music that I am happy—yes, more than happy—it is
sometimes like the bliss which is not native to this
world.'

As Mr Purcell talked thus to me, I felt a foreboding that the ardour of the spirit was too much
for his body. I prayed him to spare himself and
to regard health as the most precious gift.

' I pray you think,' I said, ' of my husband—how
deep is the trial of his state of forced inaction, due,
I believe, to the over-straining of his voice, and the
fervour with which he preached to his people at
Burton. Due, too, to long night watches by the
sick and dying, in cold, cheerless cottages, through
which the wind whistled and the rain crept through
the roof.'

' You can preach caution well, Betty,' Mr Purcell
said, with one of his sweet smiles, ' but how concerning yourself? Has not my wife cautioned you
many a time not to overtax your strength, and not
to carry little Frances out for her airings? I am
tempted to say to you, " Physician, heal thyself!"'

' Ah!' I rejoined, ' I may have been guilty in the

manner you mention, but it was the cruel, cruel shock of William Mountfort's death that has haunted me ever since. Many a time I wake shuddering in every limb, and faint with terror, as in a half-waking dream I rehearse that terrible scene and hear his dying groans.'

'Nay, nay, you do ill to dwell on that spectacle. Let us dismiss it and speak of it no more. It would seem you feel the horror of it more acutely than his widow. It was amazing to see her in the part of Belinda in "The Old Bachelor."'

'Yes,' I said; 'my husband did his utmost to dissuade her from taking the part, but in vain.'

'It is piteous to think how these actors must needs pander to the pleasure of the public, whether sick or well, merry or sorrowful. It is a misery to think of the aching hearts ofttimes hidden under the gay outside of the comic actor, and of the tragedies which are simulated on the stage, when the actor knows but too well by experience what the reality is.'

Mr Purcell was here interrupted by Madge's entrance with my babe Elizabeth in her arms, little Frances clinging to her gown.

'Madam has talked too long, sir,' she said, 'and Master Perceval craves your presence for a few minutes.'

'A hint that I am to take my departure,' Mr Purcell said. 'I dare to say you are right, Mistress Madge. Adieu! adieu!' and then, kissing his hand to me, he was gone.

'You look weary,' Madge said; 'Master Purcell has stayed too long.'

'He can never do that,' I said; 'it is a joy to me to see him.'

'It won't be a joy to me if you have a bad night; you will never be fit to go home unless you husband what little strength you have got. The children want the country air, and this babe would thrive better at Hertsbury than here.'

'Is she not thriving?' I asked anxiously. 'Give her to me.'

Little Elizabeth was not a healthy, robust babe, like her sister, and I felt I had blinded myself to the fact.

I said nothing then to Madge, but I determined to do my best to get strong enough to bear that long journey in the stage, to which I looked forward with dread.

At last the longed-for summer came, and on a fair August evening I found myself, with my two babes and my husband, at my old home.

How sweet and fresh was the country air and

the familiar sounds which fell on my ear; the
ripple of the mill stream, the caw of the rooks
near the church, the lowing of the cows come home
for the milking.

Little Frances was all alive after her long slumber
in the stage, and, holding her father's hand, trotted
down the garden path to the porch, saying, as she
looked up at the climbing roses which hung from it,—

'Pretty, pretty fowers!'

Yes, it was a sweet home-coming, and my husband gathered the servants, both outdoor and in-
door, in our little chapel, and read part of the
evening prayer, ending with the general thanksgiving. Mrs Turner and our good Joyce, old Giles
and Rhoda, were almost tearful in their welcome,
Joyce saying she never had expected to see
his reverence in that place again or hear his
voice.

'But,' she added, 'he must never try it by raising
it, or mischief will come. And as to you, dear
mistress, you and the babe look like shadows.
You must be fed with milk warm from the cow,
and cream to fatten you.'

It was wonderful to us to find how well the farm
had prospered in our absence. The yields of barley
and oats and the fruit of the orchard had been
plentiful; the cottagers on the few acres of our land

were all content, and, in truth, we were blessed in our store by the goodness of God.

It was the more surprising, as in many parts of the country the spring had been marked by the severity of the weather and the slow coming of anything like summer heat.

Of the quiet and restful year which followed our return to Ivy Farm there is little to record.

Our household was increased by a young and godly man who desired instruction in Latin and Greek and in Divinity, and who came to take up his abode with us.

My husband found it a pleasant occupation to have the training of this youth's mind, and forming, by his influence, his character.

Eustace Berkeley was no ordinary young man, and so gentle and courteous in his manner that he won all our hearts. He read in our little chapel for my husband the sermons that he wrote week by week for his people.

Madge had done her part, and, indeed, her conduct had been worthy of all praise. She had an exceeding clear, ringing voice, and she became an attraction to outsiders to frequent the chapel ; so that she asked Leonard to give orders that only our own people were to be admitted.

'Master Blankly had come,' she said, 'in a fume

one day and asked what right a woman could have to read a prayer or a lesson. Was she a mad Quakeress in fine clothing? He would have none on't.' Then Madge laughingly said, 'I have never told you he wanted none of my reading, but he wanted me to nurse his gouty leg. He did me the honour to ask me to be mistress of Burton Rectory. A likely matter, truly! I declined the honour he would have done me, and, by your leave, Betty, I mean to live with you all my life. I have no desire to be tied to any man. I like my own way, as you know.'

It often caused Leonard sorrow of heart to think that he was deprived of the suitable performance of his duties as a minister of Christ. There were many besides Mr Blankly who were ready to condemn him as contumacious and rebellious against authority by holding services in a conventicle.

'Better ask the old miller to hold forth,' Mr Blankly said one day. 'He'll roar like a bull of Bashan, and the folks will flock into your barn.'

My husband referred the matter to the deprived Bishop of Bath and Wells, Dr Ken, whose advice he had often sought before.

He replied in a letter full of godly counsel to the effect that, as an ordained minister of Christ, he had a right to administer the Holy Communion

on Sundays and festivals to his own household,
but that he was to be careful to give no occasion
to the enemy to blaspheme; and walk circumspectly
—giving offence to none by using any undue influence which might seem to draw the parishioners
of Burton from their church.

As to the little church of Hertsbury, it was now
the abode of rats and mice, while bats flew in and
out through the broken panes of the east window.

Doubtless the rector who held it with two other
rich benefices was guilty of gross neglect. But
no one called him to account—he living in a distant county; and though, when he first held these
benefices in my youth, a curate lived in a small cottage hard by, by degrees this had dropped to a
visitation thrice in the year, and now the village
was deserted, so far as the Church was concerned.

This holding of pluralities was a sore blot on the
conduct of those in authority in the Church. Small
wonder that Papists and Nonconformists, Quakers,
Puritans and the like came to districts deserted like
Hertsbury, and gained the hearts of the people, who
were in good truth as sheep without a shepherd.

The year 1694 was one of peace and plenty to us.

Our children were a source of continual pleasure,
and little Elizabeth opened like a flower in sunshine in her country home.

My husband also gathered strength in the atmosphere which surrounded him, and Eustace Berkeley was as a younger brother to us.

He was an orphan under the care of a somewhat tyrannical guardian, and he was happy to find his home with us.

During this year, as I look back on it, I ask myself had I any crosses to bear or any troubles to mar my bliss. I think I can say with a thankful heart that the motto of this year may be written thus for me,—

'He maketh peace in thy borders, and filleth thee with the flour of wheat.'

Towards the end of September my heart was sad for my dear friends in Dean's Yard.

Mrs Purcell was not swift with her pen, and her letters were few and short; but I could see, when I received one in the autumn of this year, that her anxieties for my dear master were many and great.

'He looks often weary, and cannot take sufficient rest,' she said. 'He is up late, and often returns in the chill night air coughing terribly. It is vain for me to entreat him to be careful and spare himself. He is more than ever at the beck and call of rhymesters and playwrights, nobles and great folk, and gives himself scarce a moment's quiet or rest. My little Mary, our last born, is an ailing child and I fear we shall never see her, like her sister and brother, happy and healthful.'

This letter made me reply by begging Mrs Purcell to bring the little one with her, and let me see her flourish as my own Elizabeth had done in pure air and with milk warm from the cow for her morning meal.

Leonard was always ready to agree with any plan I wished to carry out, and he said,—

'The house is yours, dear wife, and you are free to fill it as you please.'

I never liked to hear Leonard say this, and told him he forgot that what was mine was his, and it hurt me that he should speak of this, and before witnesses, for Madge was present, and was conning a page of Virgil with Eustace Berkeley.

Madge could always turn everything into a jest, and looking up from her book she said,—

'Betty owns nothing but the harpsichord and her spinning-wheel—ah! and I forgot, her goose quill. She would not care if the house were burnt down if she could keep these her favourite goods and chattels.'

'And how concerning the children?' Leonard asked.

'Ah, I forgot the children. They are not goods and chattels, they are the apples of Betty's eyes.'

'And do I count for naught?' Leonard said, laughing.

'To be sure you do. She is bone of your bone, and flesh of your flesh. There! I can't say any more, or I shall never get through this line.'

'Yes,' I said, 'Madge, you must say more. Will you think Mistress Purcell's and the ailing child's presence too burdensome?'

'I!—no. I do not love Mistress Purcell. I think she spoils her brats, and being a spoiled child myself, I can pity them. For,' turning to Eustace, 'I would have you know that I was the veriest little vixen and ill-behaved child that ever lived.'

Eustace laughed.

'What, then, has made you a well-behaved young gentlewoman? You must have vastly changed, if what you say is true.'

Madge rose, and making a deep curtsey, said, in a mocking tone, to Eustace,—

'I give you humble thanks for your good opinion of me, sir; and as to *what* has changed me, I will tell you. You must ask *who*, not *what*, and I answer, this gentlewoman who disclaims ownership of this house, but she cannot disclaim the fact that she has for her own the love and respect of everyone in it. There's a fine speech for you,' she said. 'Why, Betty, what ails you?' for, overcome with a sense of my unworthiness to hear these words, I left the parlour to hide my tears.

Madge was after me in a moment.

'It is true, Betty! it is true!' and flinging her arms round me with all her old, passionate fervour, she said, 'You make everyone who lives with you love you.'

I scarce like to record this, save to show that a wild nature like dear Madge's can only be won by love and tenderness. The rule of school had prepared the way for the rule of love, not, as I hope, unmixed with firmness, which I held over her.

Madge may never read what I have written here; indeed, as I write, I often wonder who will read the records of my life. Most like they will be hid away in some bureau or chest, and lie unheeded. I shall never speak of them or tell my children of their existence. I should not care to have this history read in my lifetime. When I am dead those who survive me may chance to find it, and whatsoever there may be in it which is approved, or is thought dull and prosy, can then meet what it deserves, whether of praise or blame.

Mrs Purcell and her child were welcome in our happy household. If more labour fell on Madge and our good Mrs Turner and Joyce, they never murmured.

And I confess it was a pleasure to me to sit with my spinning-wheel while Mrs Purcell gave me news of the great world, from which I seemed now as far distant as if I lived in the Indies.

Then I would sit down to the harpsichord and do my best to play the late compositions of Mr Purcell, copies of which he had sent me.

The *Te Deum* and *Jubilate* for the festival of St Cecilia were beyond measure beautiful, and I grieved to be unable to render them as they ought to have been rendered. Then there was the birthday ode for the little Duke of Gloucester, which, Mrs Purcell said, had won great praise from the Princess Anne.

Mrs Purcell had been several times commanded to appear with her husband at Whitehall, and had been treated with great condescension by the Queen and the Princess Anne.

'There can be no question,' Mrs Purcell said, 'that the Queen wins all hearts, and by her sweetness and gentleness atones for the King's morose and sullen temper.'

'I wish,' I said, 'I could forget that she was cruel to her own father and allowed herself to hearken to the foolish story about the Prince of Wales.'

'I see you are a Jacobite to the backbone,' Mrs Purcell said; 'for my part, I think you had done well to persuade your husband to take the oaths of allegiance.'

'How could I persuade him to do what I myself know to be wrong?' I said.

And then we passed from any subject of dispute to speak of our children, Mrs Purcell complaining somewhat of her Edward's rebellious temper one moment, and the next saying he was a prodigy as to music, and, his father said, would excel him. Then there was not a child to compare with her Frances for beauty and wit, and if it were not for the grandmother's ill management of her, she would have been as good as she was lovely. Little Mary was daily growing stronger, and it was a pretty sight to watch our Frances playing with her and patiently bearing the fretful pining which is ever the sign of a child's want of health.

Sometimes, when I heard Mrs Purcell extolling her children, I wondered if I erred in the same way, for, after all is said, praising one's children is praising oneself.

Yet dearly as Leonard and I loved our little daughters, I do not think we over-indulged them, but did our best to train them in the ways of obedience and truth, without the rod, which is a favourite punishment with many parents.

Much that Mrs Purcell said of Susanna Mountfort gave Leonard uneasiness. She was so bound up with the life of the stage that the loss of her noble husband was apparently forgotten. I would say apparently, for which of us can find out the spirit of others or gauge their feelings, whether of joy or sorrow?

I liked almost less to hear of the warmth of friendship between Mrs Bracegirdle and young Mr Congreve.

'Every play he writes,' Mrs Purcell said, 'has a character made expressly for her. Doubtless, Araminta, in "The Old Bachelor," made Mistress Bracegirdle famous, or rather increased her fame. Now the Queen's liking for "The Double Dealer," and admiration of Cynthia, has brought Mistress Bracegirdle royal favour, and she is more run after than ever. There are sharp tongues which are busy about her friendship with Master Congreve, but there have always been folk jealous of her, who have done their best to defame her character.

As we spoke of these matters, we little imagined how soon the theatres would be closed and the whole kingdom plunged in mourning.

Mrs Purcell and her babe departed under care of Eustace Berkeley, who was summoned to an interview with his guardian towards the middle of November.

He brought back bad news of the vast increase of the smallpox, and the terror it caused in all parts of London.   Having a lively remembrance of the fearful condition of poor Adelicia's face, I could scarce be surprised that there was a panic amongst the gentlewomen at Court lest it should reach Kensington Palace, where the Queen was now residing.

One dark night there was the sound of horses' feet and a loud knocking at the door, and to the question called out by old Giles, 'Who goes there?' we heard Edmund Pelham's voice shouting his own name in loud tones.

He came into the house drenched with rain and shivering in every limb.   Leonard went to him, and found him in abject terror lest he had caught the dreaded malady.

Leonard spoke sharply to him, and bid him remember that fear was the sure road to catch the disease.   And so it proved.   The hurried ride from London in the rain brought on what was maybe lying dormant in him.

Leonard, although far above any weak fears for himself, remembered the danger to his household, and more especially to me and to our children.   He was sorely perplexed what to do.

It was hard not to feel contempt for a man who

stricken with the fear of contagion for himself, could come to risk developing the dread disease in the house of a friend.

Eustace and my husband took counsel together, and decided that though Edmund could not be refused the night's shelter, he could not be suffered to remain under our roof.

The difficulty was solved the next day by the readiness of the old miller Joe to serve us. When Eustace told him of our dilemma he said he had neither chick nor child, and his old serving-maid had, like himself, gone through the disease years before.

Now Edmund showed his selfish disregard of others' welfare by making objections to being sent to the mill.

But Madge delivered herself to so much purpose, and without any reserve, to Edmund, that he consented to remove to the mill, taking his servant with him, and leaving his horses stabled with ours,

His fears that he had caught the smallpox were but too well founded. Within a week he was laid in the grave by his wife ; thus closed the sad story of two lives which had opened with fair promise, blighted by the breath of the world and sinful disregard of all that was pure and of good report.

By God's mercy there was no other victim in

T

Hertsbury and Burton, and the kindness of old Joe, and his readiness to help us in our time of need, showed us, if we needed a proof, that Christian faith and practice are not tied to any precise form.

Deeply attached as we were to the Church in which my husband was a minister, we, from this time, may be, could look with kindlier eye on those who had separated from her. Verily, God is no respecter of persons.

Only those who can recall the Christmastide of this year, and but few are now left, can believe the shock of sorrow and distress which the death of the Queen caused throughout the kingdom. She was beloved in life, but she was even more beloved in her death.

Her heroic conduct when she found herself stricken with this dreaded scourge was seen by her command that all her attendants and ladies should leave Kensington Palace who had not suffered from smallpox. Thus but few remained. But now, as is often seen, the husband, who had to all seeming been cold and even faithless to his wife, was overcome with a mighty grief, terrible to witness.

In vain the Queen besought him to leave her. He would not do so. He had his little pallet bed brought to her chamber, and there he lay to watch and hope against hope.

So bitter was his grief when at last, on the 29th day of December, the Queen died, that the physician feared for the result. Of him it might indeed be said his soul refused comfort.

Great preparations were made for the funeral, which was to exceed in show and pomp any that had preceded it since the funeral of that great knight who fell after the fight at Zutphen—Sir Philip Sidney.

The burial was long delayed, and it was considered by many a great risk to the lives of survivors, but every precaution was taken, and no evil consequences ensued.

We heard tidings of the conduct of many of the Jacobite clergymen, which was painful to Leonard. Although a Non-Juror for conscience' sake, none deplored the early death of the Queen more sincerely, and he reproved Eustace with some severity one day when he spoke of a righteous judgment falling on all undutiful daughters.

Madge, always quick to take up an argument, now said,—

'I don't put faith in judgments, for I am a living instance that they don't fall on the right head. Ask Betty whether I was a dutiful daughter. She knows I was not, and no judgment has fallen on me, for here I am, as happy and prosperous as heart could

wish, No, no ; judgments do not always follow undutiful behaviour.'

Eustace laughed, saying,—

'You are very prone to hit yourself with sharp
arrows, while you rise up in wrath if anyone dare
so much as to point one at you.'

This was true, and true of us all. It is easy to
confess faults, sometimes, as I have known, in the
expectation that those to whom we are speaking
will deny the justice of our self-condemnation.
There is too often a want of sincerity in these ap-
peals to others concerning our particular faults and
shortcomings. Thus, when Madge said, ' Ask Betty
if I were a dutiful daughter,' I shook my head, and,
in a voice which reached her ear, if not Eustace
Berkeley's, I answered her question with ' No.'

BOOK VII

1695

Music to hear, why hear'st thou music sadly?
  Sweets with sweets war not, joy delights in joy.
Why lov'st thou that which thou receiv'st not gladly?
  Or else receiv'st with pleasure thine annoy?
  .   .   .   .

Mark, how one string, sweet husband to another,
  Strikes each in each, by mutual ordering.
Resembling sire and child and happy mother,
  Who all in one, one pleasing note do sing.
SHAKESPEARE, Sonnets (VIII).

CHAPTER XIII

A.D. 1695

IT was on the 5th day of March of this year that
Queen Mary was buried.

We heard from Eustace Berkeley—who, with the
curiosity of youth and love of a grand spectacle,
had been present in the Abbey—the account of
an eye-witness of the great ceremony. The chief
interest for me centred in hearing that the anthems
composed for the occasion by Mr Purcell were
considered the finest he had ever written.

Even Eustace, who was not very easily moved
by music, said that when the words, 'Thou
knowest, Lord, the secrets of our hearts; shut not
Thy merciful ears to our prayer,' were sung, he
felt tears raining down his face, and that almost
everyone was weeping.

Such music for a funeral, he said, was never heard
before. The rest of the mournful pageant only

made me think, as Eustace described it, how a simple burial, without all this pomp and show, is far more in accord with the feelings of sorrow in the hearts of those who are bereaved.

The waxen effigy of the poor Queen, dressed in all her grand attire of velvet and jewels, placed outside her coffin, filled me with distress, yet Eustace said there had been a vast throng of people of all kinds and degrees who pressed to get a view of this figure as Queen Mary lay in state. Moreover, that the King had ordered the figure to be executed, and seemed to consider it one of the chief honours which he desired to heap on the memory of his dead wife.

In answer to my inquiry concerning Mr Purcell, Eustace said he had scarce seen him.

He had, in obedience to my wish, been to Dean's Yard, and old Mrs Purcell spoke of her son as very much troubled with a cough, and said that he would not spare himself, and what with his work for the Abbey and the Chapel Royal, and the many compositions on which he was engaged, and the grand people who were constantly sending for him, she was certain he was wearing himself to death.

I knew that his mother always took the worst view of the dear master's health, and was prone to look on the dark side of most people and things, as is common with the aged, and from which I pray for the sake of others to be preserved.

Yet I was filled with uneasiness about my dear master, for whom time and absence had not chilled my affection or the admiration I had ever felt for him and his marvellous genius.

I had a longing to go to London to see for myself the condition of my best friend, for such I must ever consider Mr Purcell to be.

But the birth of our little son in March, who came to crown the happiness of our home, prevented me from fulfilling this desire for some months. Moreover, our harvest this year was very scanty, and it may be said that the month of August was one of extraordinary severity. Frosts at night were very severe, and then torrents of cold rain.

This inclement weather affected Leonard's health, and he was mostly confined to the house, and yet he never murmured or was cross-grained. He was cheerful and happy with his books, his writing, and, above all, with his children.

Little Frances was an exceeding clever child, and knew her horn book before she was five. She had also a wonderful memory, and could recite long passages from the Scriptures at her father's bidding.

She had also a gift for mimicry, and when she recited she had graceful actions with her little hands.

'Born to be an actress,' Mrs Draper, a neighbour, said one day when the child had recited a verse of Mr Milton's Christmas hymn in her presence.

'God forbid!' I exclaimed.

'Well-a-day, Mistress Perceval,' was the rejoinder. 'The child must needs have inherited her gifts from her grandfather, Master Perceval, and her aunt, Mistress Mountfort.'

'Mistress Mountfort is not Frances's aunt,' I replied, with some heat; 'Susanna is my husband's cousin. They were brought up together, and hence the mistake which is often made.'

'Well, for my part,' my neighbour, Mrs Draper, exclaimed, 'had I a daughter, I should be proud to see her courted and admired, like Mistress Bracegirdle, but many folks say you are a Puritan at heart, Mistress Perceval.'

Mrs Draper was a busybody, and too ready to pry into matters that did not concern her, and to give her opinion unsought. But her words filled me with anxiety, and I did not suffer my Frances to recite before witnesses for some time in consequence.

As I had often thought likely, Eustace Berkeley

became the lover of Madge. She, on her part, was often sharper with her tongue to him than I thought seemly, nor could I be sure whether she favoured his suit or not.

My husband spoke sincerely to Eustace, and said he could not suffer him to proceed with his suit without informing his guardian. Eustace was to come in for a fortune when he reached twenty-one, and Madge was, save for what we could do for her, penniless.

This determination of Leonard's, that Eustace should see his guardian, brought matters to a point.

I did my best to find out what Madge really felt, and after much fencing and attempts at pretending she was indifferent to Eustace, I was angry with Madge, and said I would have no more coquetting and folly, smiling one moment and frowning the next. Madge only laughed, and said everyone had not a soft heart like mine, nor a sweet temper neither. She did not think she would ever wed, and if I was sick of her she would go and earn her bread in the world.

Then, seeing I was much displeased and even tearful at her words, Madge threw herself, in her old, passionate way, on the floor by my side, saying, with sobs, that she loved me and the children, and would die for us if needs must, but she did not wish Eustace to bind himself to her, who had no fortune, while he might pick and choose some fine lady who would bring him something beside her face and a quick temper and a strong will.

After much consultation and thought, Leonard and I decided that Eustace should leave Ivy Farm for a time at least, and that his guardian should be informed that it would be of use to him to travel and see the world before presenting himself for Holy Orders, which was his greatest desire.

It was just after we had come to this decision that I had a few words from Mrs Purcell which filled me with sorrow. She begged me to go to her — for Mr Purcell was very ill, and he craved for my presence.

I scarce knew how to ask Leonard to let me go, and when he saw me weeping he said,—

'What ails you, sweetheart?'

I gave him Mrs Purcell's letter, and he said,—

'Well, here is a chance of Eustace's safe conduct; you shall go to your poor friend.'

'Oh!' I said, 'it is hard to leave you and the babes. I am in a great strait. I know not whether to go or stay.'

'I will settle this matter for you, Betty; you shall go to comfort one who was a friend to you when you were in need of one; and as to the babes, what with our good Joyce and Madge, they will be well cared for.'

So it was settled, and on the All Saints' Festival I set forth once more in the stage for London. To leave all I loved so well was hard, but more especially my little son, who, though a well-favoured and healthy boy, was more like my delicate Elizabeth than Frances.

'I'll tend baby brother,' Frances said when she clung to my neck. 'I'll be a good girl. Do not weep, mother.'

Dear child! how she strove to smile at me through her tears as I left the porch. My baby Henry, cooing and crowing in Madge's arms all unconscious of my departure, and Elizabeth intent on eating a sweet cake Joan had given her, I noticed as I looked back that Madge had hidden her face in my little babe's neck after waving her good-bye, and saying in a choked voice, '*Bon voyage*,' to Eustace. He, poor fellow was trying to put a good face on the separation, but his woe-begone aspect made me say,—

'You must take heart, Eustace, and let us look for a happy return and meeting with those we love.'

'If only I was sure that she cared for me.'

I do not know whether it was well said, but I replied,—

'I think she does care for you. Did you not see her tears at parting?'

'Tears at your loss,' he said gloomily, 'not for mine.'

I could not say more; my own heart was heavy with the grief of parting from Leonard. I would not suffer him to come forth in the chill air of early morning to see me off to the stage. We said our farewells in our little chapel where prayer was wont to be made.

Once more in Dean's Yard, after an absence of two years! It was too dark to see the Abbey walls, and there was a clinging mist which hid all but near objects from sight.

But presently the familiar chime of the Abbey clock struck on my ear like the voice of welcome, and brought to me the old message of peace.

Eustace left me at the door, which was quickly opened in answer to our knock. In the entrance, under the lamp, I saw Edward and Frances, who ran out to meet me, crying out,—

'Aunt Bet is come! Aunt Bet is come!'

To my amazement, Mr Purcell's voice sounded from the parlour.

'Come in, come in, Betty!'

I hastened to my dear master, and saw him leaning back in his chair, a table before him, on which were sheets of music.

'Ah! Betty. I am in *Rosie Bowers*, despite the fact that it is November and all roses are dead,' he said with a smile. 'But I get tired even of *Rosie Bowers*. Mayhap it is my swan's song. Run, children, run and summon your mother; say our dear Betty is here.'

The children scampered off to do their father's bidding, and Mr Purcell held out his hand to me. It was white and thin, and as I pressed it to my lips I felt it was burning hot.

'It was selfish to bring you here, Betty, yet I confess I wished to see you once more—once more. I do my best to seem better for my wife's sake, but I know well enough that I lose strength daily. Yet I live in a fair dreamland of sweet melodies and I have naught to complain of, though,' he said, with a far-away, wistful look in his beautiful eyes, 'I have achieved so little—and life is short, too short. I could have done more—and done better—but God's will be my will.'

'You have achieved so much,' I said, 'my dear master. Think how your music will sound on and on, and win the love of hundreds and thousands in the time to come.'

Mr Purcell's eyes lighted with joy as I said this.

'That is a good thought, Betty; thank you for it.'

Mrs Purcell now came in with little Mary in her arms, and as I took the child from her she kissed me lovingly.

'Welcome, Betty, welcome!' and then she seemed like to break down into weeping. So I said,—

'Show me to my chamber, for I would fain lay aside my warm cloak and make my hair smooth.'

I tried to speak lightly, and it was not till we were together in the bed-chamber that Mrs Purcell said, throwing herself on my neck,—

'He is dying, Betty, he is dying; he knows it, for he desires to make his will and is saying farewell to the world. Sometimes,' she said with a sudden change of mood—'sometimes I think he is better, and then my hope is kindled, and again my heart sinks when I hear his cough—often all night, nor ceasing till the dawn. 'To think of his children fatherless and of myself a widow! Betty, it is like to kill me with grief; but your husband has got well, and Henry may yet live.'

'Not well,' I said. 'Leonard is not well; but with care I may hope to keep him for many years.'

'Ah! with care,' Mrs Purcell said; 'but how can I

take the care I would of Henry? He will have the music-sheets before him—he will see the choristers, and hear them rehearse. Even now he has written a song which, when I heard it played by Mr D'Urfey, I could well believe nothing could excel for beauty and grace.'

It seemed, and indeed it was, a consolation to Mrs Purcell to talk thus to me—to tell of all her alternate hopes and fears, and I was, I love to think, a presence in the house which was welcome to my dear master.

Many came and went in these last days of Mr Purcell's life—the great and the noble; those who had listened to his music; those who loved him as a friend. The stream of sympathy flowed unceasingly toward him, and though he grew daily weaker, and could not see any but Mr Gostling and a few chosen friends, he liked to know that he was remembered by the hundreds who came to the door to ask how it fared with him.

It fell to me to see many who came to the house and answer questions which Mr Purcell's aged mother could not find courage to answer.

The Dean and prebendaries; the theatrical folk, and amongst them Mr Congreve, Susanna Mountfort and her father, were frequently at the door.

Not Mrs Bracegirdle. I sometimes wondered at

U

her absence, and I felt certain it was not from lack of feeling. I learned afterwards that she was greatly troubled at this time about the intimacy existing between her and Mr Congreve, and that my dear master had bid her be careful not to give a colour to the scandalmongers, hovering like evil birds ready for their prey. Mr Congreve had made Mrs Bracegirdle his idol—so much I knew— nor do I greatly care to know precisely what their relations were; and thus I leave that beautiful woman, who, in the first enthusiasm of youth, I well-nigh worshipped, and of whose purity and deeds of blessed charity to the sick, the sinful and the sad, there could then be no shadow of doubt.

The twenty-first day of November, the eve of the festival of St Cecilia, dawned in gloom.

Mr Purcell did not attempt to take his pen in hand, or raise himself from his couch.

At his request a lawyer was called in, and wrote from his lips his last will and testament. It was duly signed in the presence of two witnesses, and was a last act to show his perfect confidence in, and love for, his wife, for he left her sole executrix, giving and bequeathing to her all he possessed.

This done, there fell a stillness over the house. The children were awestruck, and, at their father's request, were in his chamber as the end drew on.

WESTMINSTER ABBEY, FROM DEAN'S YARD, IN THE SEVENTEENTH CENTURY.

The bell for evensong sounded, and Mr Purcell's face shone with a strange light as he said,—

'This is the eve of St Cecilia. How I have loved that day!'

He was in the full possession of his faculties to the last.

In the silence of all around we could catch the faint roll of the organ in the Abbey, never again to answer to the touch of the master's hand.

I am sure he heard it, for presently he raised his hand and said,—

'Hearken! Those are the words of the Psalm— the last words, "Blessed be the Lord God of Israel." Yes, yes, "let all the people say amen." Say amen, sweet wife. Say amen, dear mother.'

There was no sound of weeping. How could we disturb the peace of the dying with wail of earthly sorrow?

'Amen, amen,' came in clear tones from the lips he loved best in the world, and little Edward and Frances said 'amen.'

He did not speak again, and as the last faint murmur of the organ died away, the spirit of the master had passed hence, where the music of the heavenly choirs greeted him who had filled earth with the melodies which are as a link between this world and another.

It were vain for me to put down in words the effect upon the vast crowd gathered together in the Abbey on the twenty-sixth day of November, when Mr Purcell was buried under the organ which now sent forth the music of the anthems written but a few short months ago for the funeral of the Queen, and now sung over the grave of him who had composed them.

The wintry sun came aslant across the nave, piercing the mist which had filled the Abbey, and as the procession passed along a ray of light illumined the coffin ere it was lowered out of sight.

The words of the anthem, ' Thou knowest, Lord, the secrets of our hearts,' were accompanied by low, mournful, yet majestic sounds of trumpets.

Every head in that vast throng was bowed with sorrow, every heart thrilled with grief, as it was remembered that never again would the master's hand touch the keys of the organ, and that the place of one so well loved and honoured would know him no more.

There never was a moment in my life such as this.

Stirred by the heavenly strain, my spirit, too often earth-bound, seemed to rise to those blessed realms where songs of praise had no note of earthly sadness to mar their beauty.

Uplifted by the majestic music as it soared above me to the vaulted roof of the Abbey, I was fain to realise the bliss of him who was free from the burden of the flesh and was filled with the harmonies of celestial music in the presence of God.

As we passed through the cloister to the house left desolate in Dean's Yard, I caught sight of a face on which was written sorrow, and a wistful look as of one who was weary of the world and longed for rest.

Beautiful exceedingly was the face, but what I read there in a passing glance haunted me, ay, and haunts me still.

It was the last time I ever looked on Anne Bracegirdle.

I stayed in Dean's Yard to be of what comfort I could to my dear master's widow and children, and his aged mother, who was borne down with her grief.

Mrs Purcell had a brave if sore heart; she roused herself from unavailing laments, and set herself to do all that was possible to honour her husband's memory.

She set about collecting Mr Purcell's compositions, and pleased herself by writing dedications to the works which were full of the devoted affection she bore him as his wife and admiration for his great gifts.

These works were published in the year which followed, and were received with enthusiasm by the musicians who maybe had never fully known what a genius they had amongst them till they lost him. He was only thirty-seven when he died.

Christmastide found me once more in my own home, where I was gladdened by the sweet welcome awaiting me there, and I never before gave thanks, as I did the day of my return, for the blessings of my home. Maybe this was by reason of the contrast afforded by the desolation of that other home I had just quitted, and the happiness of that to which I had come.

As I look back on the years which have passed since that Christmastide, I do not see in them much to record, for the calm and peaceful life of home does not afford any startling events, and an old woman is apt to get prosy and to put undue importance on the details of past days.

I may take up my quill again, but I scarce think I shall do so, and I am very sure I shall have naught to tell of anyone I may have seen and known in later years who can compare with him whom I still love to think of as my dear master—who, from the day when good Mr Gostling took me to his house to the day when he passed hence, was my dear and honoured friend. His memory does not fade, his music lives, and one of the dear delights of my old age is to hear it, as my grandchild, Frances, with her gift of song, makes the old parlour ring with some of the strains which are to me as a message from past years and the voice of the great musician, Henry Purcell.

NOTE

By Elizabeth Perceval's Grand-daughter,
Frances Melville

THE history of my dear grandmother, Elizabeth
Perceval, has been gathered together and arranged
by me, the daughter of her much-loved child,
Frances, who, dying at my birth, left me an
orphan, for my father fell fighting for the Jacobite
cause in 1715.

My grandmother left me Ivy Farm and all that
appertained to it, and it has been my desire to
fulfil her wishes, as much as in me lies, and follow
in her steps.

Hers was a beautiful old age; and who could live
with her and not own her influence, and strive to
follow her example?

She mentioned to me several times that in a
small oaken chest I should find some records of
her early life. But she desired that they should

not see the light till everyone who, perchance, might take umbrage at aught that she had said had passed away.

For a long time my search for these papers was fruitless, and I began to despair of finding them, when one day Madge Berkeley's little son, rummaging in the garret for apples, came running to me with a small box in his hands, on which were carved the letters L. B. P.

The child could scarce carry it, and let it fall just as he reached my chair. The lid flew open, and out fell a mass of papers, yellow with age, and with delight I found them to be the history of my grandmother's young days, of which she had spoken to me. It was the labour of some months to copy and put the manuscript in order. Now it is done, and if a labour, it has been a labour of love. I have changed nothing in the narrative, save here and there to fill in a space with a word which might seem appropriate. As will be seen, thè story told by my grandmother ends abruptly in 1695.

There were but few more pages, and these were mostly concerning the joys and sorrows of her uneventful life — the births and deaths of several children, and the success of her son Henry, who was named after the great musician, for whom my grandmother entertained the most devoted affection throughout her long life.

The mention of my grandfather's death is affecting in its simple pathos. She wrote of it in few words, thus,—

'The great sorrow of my life fell on me this Easter day of 1708. My husband then passed through the grave and gate of death, and left me a widow, and desolate. I can say no more of this grief, it is too deep for words. My children rise up to comfort me, and I give thanks that they have known such a father.'

My Aunt Elizabeth made a rich marriage, and so did my Uncle Henry.

Their position and affluence being secured, my grandmother felt no scruple in leaving me this house, where I am now writing.

Nor do any of my kindred grudge me the comforts of a home hallowed with the memories of one who was my very dearest and best friend, and who was, indeed, more than a mother to me.

Let no one think that my grandmother lacked cheerfulness, or was sad and melancholy in speech and behaviour, because in these records of her life she has to tell of the sorrows which fall to the lot of everyone, with but few exceptions, in this changing world.

Of my grandmother it may be said her light shone more and more unto the perfect day. She had ever a bright smile of welcome for all who came to Ivy Farm, always a cheery word, always leisure to rejoice with the joyful, and I sometimes think this is more difficult than to sympathise with the sorrowful.

The young loved her, and brought much pleasure into her latter years. The Madge often mentioned in this history never passed a year without coming hither with one or more of her children, and she loved my grandmother with what I may call a passionate devotion.

As Ivy Farm (or Manor, as my Uncle Henry prefers to style it, now he is risen in the world) was ever open in my grandmother's lifetime to her children and children's children, so I desire to keep it now. If any are sick and ailing, they come hither for country air, and they are welcome.

A single life like mine has its charm, and I have never wished to change my estate, for reasons which, without entering into personal details of a now far-off time, I cannot give.

That all my grandmother's descendants may have a true picture of her, drawn by her own hand, is my desire, and if that desire is fulfilled I shall reap a rich reward.

Her death was like her life—peaceful and full of faith. Westminster Abbey she was wont to call 'the home of her spirit,' and it is remarkable that in her last hours she believed herself to be there, again and again asking me if I did not hear the chimes of the Abbey, the lovely strains of the organ, and the voices of the choir. In dying ears there is often the sound of music—the music which those who are standing by hear not.

It was at daybreak, by a strange coincidence, on the eve of St Cecilia's day, that my grandmother departed in peace, as on that very day one whom she ever loved to call her master—Henry Purcell— entered into his rest.

FRANCES MELVILLE.

Written at her house of
Ivy Farm, on the first day
of October, A.D. 1750.

THE END

Colston and Coy. Limited, Printers, Edinburgh